ALL THE PRESIDENT'S MEN?

# ALL THE PRESIDENT'S MEN?

Scenes from the Senate Confirmation
Hearings of President Trump's cabinet

Edited by Nicolas Kent

OBERON BOOKS
LONDON

WWW.OBERONBOOKS.COM

First published in 2017 by Oberon Books Ltd
521 Caledonian Road, London N7 9RH
Tel: +44 (0) 20 7607 3637 / Fax: +44 (0) 20 7607 3629
e-mail: info@oberonbooks.com
www.oberonbooks.com

A catalogue record for this book is available from the British
Library.

PB ISBN: 9781786822116
E ISBN: 9781786822123

Cover photo by Gage Skidmore
creativecommons.org/licenses

Printed and bound by 4edge Limited, Essex, UK.
eBook conversion by CPI Group (UK) Ltd, Croydon, CR0 4YY.

Visit www.oberonbooks.com to read more about all our books
and to buy them. You will also find features, author interviews and
news of any author events, and you can sign up for e-newsletters
so that you're always first to hear about our new releases.

*For*

Jenifer Landor

Belinda Lang

and Nicola Russell

whose love and care was a huge support during the making
of this play, and who certainly know the meaning of "truth".

## Acknowledgements

In America: I am enormously grateful to Liz Frankel without whose encouragement I might never have pursued the idea of this play, to the friendship and inspiration of Oskar Eustis of the Public Theater who made it possible, then wholeheartedly embraced it and ensured that his wonderful producing team of Maria Goyanes, Jeanie O'Hare and Yuvika Tolani gave me the support to bring it from page to stage.

In London: I am grateful for the continuing support of the National Theatre under the adventurous guidance of Rufus Norris and Ben Power who, once again, bravely said yes to a difficult project on an impossible time-scale. To Sacha Milroy producing with her usual flair and for being undaunted by that time-scale. To Erica Campayne for being my dedicated line producer. And to Nica Burns of Nimax for running with the idea, generously giving us The Vaudeville Theatre, and proving once more to be such a trusted and loyal friend.

I am also very indebted to Jack Bradley, Bonnie Capes, James Hogan, Kate Loewald, Blanche Marvin and Hal Scardino for their steadfast advice and encouragement.

Finally I have to thank Charlotte Westenra for spending much of February and March helping to type numerous drafts, making valuable suggestions for cuts and revisions, and for her endless optimism and dedication to the project – she made working to this time-scale possible and the play much better.

*Nicolas Kent, 3rd April 2017*

# Foreword

The Senate confirmation hearing process started ten days before Donald Trump's inauguration, and none of the appointments were confirmed until after he became President. Most of the major Cabinet appointments were confirmed at the end of January and during February 2017.

The President's nominees being confirmed submit background papers for a vetting process prior to appearing at a public Senate committee hearing conducted by the relevant committee for their particular Cabinet post (for instance the Senate Foreign Relations committee for the nominee for Secretary of State). These committees have a Chairman who is from the majority party and a Ranking Member who is the lead for the opposition party. Most of the committees in this play comprised between eight-twelve members with a Republican Chairman, and with a majority of one over the Democrats.

After the first hearing, which usually lasts somewhere between four to nine hours, further statements, clarifications, or other character witnesses are often called. Sometimes the nominee is recalled. At the end of this first process, the committee reconvenes some days later to vote on the confirmation of the candidate. This vote is then a recommendation to the Senate before the candidate is confirmed (or not confirmed) by a vote of the full Senate. It is very unusual for a committee not to recommend a nominee of a newly installed President, and equally unusual for the full Senate to reject the recommendation of one of its committees.

The hearings themselves often follow the precedent of the previous administration's process – although the details are subject to some negotiation between the opposition party and the Chairman of the committee. The Chairman briefly welcomes and introduces the nominee. The nominee then has a number of proposers who speak about him or her – they are usually, but not always, members or ex-members of Congress. After that the Chairman and Ranking Member speak about the suitability of the nominee, the nominee then makes their opening statement which is followed by the Chairman and Ranking Member commenting upon it and asking their first round of questions. There are then two or three or even four rounds of time-limited questions from each member of the committee – usually alternating between the Senators from opposing parties.

Often the nominee has already visited each committee Senator in their office on Capitol Hill during the weeks preceding the hearing in order to lay out their stall.

This play has chosen to focus on the confirmation hearings of the four candidates that are in many ways going to most define the Trump presidency domestically and world-wide. The four hearings comprised well over twenty-four of hours of testimony, so the play represents less than 10% of those hearings.

Much has inevitably been left out, including many Senators and their questions, much in the nominees' statements and all of their proposers' statements. But the order of the questioning is strictly chronological, and every question gets the answer it received (although both the question & answer have often been edited for length). Any text in square [brackets] has been added to the verbatim for the purposes of clarity for the reader, and was not actually spoken.

Finally I have tried to be as impartial and fair as possible in this editing process, but inevitably most of the questioning comes from the Senate Democrats because, as the opposition party, their role is one of trying to pose the sort of questions which elicit the most revealing answers – and the function of this play is to try to lay bear, as much as possible, the philosophy, character and policy ideals of the new Trump administration.

*Nicolas Kent, 3rd April 2017*

# Characters

Nominees:

| | | |
|---|---|---|
| | Rex Tillerson | Ex CEO ExxonMobil |
| | Dr Tom Price | Congressman |
| | Scott Pruitt | Alabama Attorney General |
| | Jeff Sessions | Senator for Alabama |

Panel Members:
Senator Bob Corker
Senator Benjamin L. Cardin
Senator Marco Rubio
Senator Robert Menendez
Senator Ron Johnson
Senator Tim Kaine
Senator Todd Young
Senator Lamar Alexander
Senator Patty Murray
Senator Bernard Sanders
Senator Orrin G. Hatch
Senator Al Franken
Senator Michael Bennet
Senator Sheldon Whitehouse
Senator Christopher S. Murphy
Senator Elizabeth Warren
Senator John Barrasso
Senator Thomas R. Carper
Senator James M. Inhofe
Senator Jeff Merkley
Senator Edward J. Markey
Senator Charles E. Grassley
Senator Patrick J. Leahy
Senator Lindsey Graham
Senator Richard J. Durbin
Senator Chris Coons
Senator Ted Cruz
Senator Mazie K. Hirono
Senator Dianne Feinstein

Protesters:     Various

Setting: various Senate Committee meeting rooms on Capitol Hill.

# National Theatre

The National Theatre makes world-class theatre that is entertaining, challenging and inspiring. And we make it for everyone.

We stage up to thirty productions at our South Bank home each year, ranging from reimagined classics – such as Greek tragedy and Shakespeare – to modern masterpieces and new work by contemporary writers and theatremakers.

The work we make strives to be as open, as diverse, as collaborative and as national as possible. Much of that new work is researched and developed at the NT Studio: we are committed to nurturing innovative work from new writers, directors, creative artists and performers. Equally, we are committed to education, with a wide-ranging Learning programme for all ages in our Clore Learning Centre and in schools and communities across the UK.

The National's work is also seen on tour throughout the UK and internationally, and in collaborations and co-productions with regional theatres. Popular shows transfer to the West End and occasionally to Broadway. Through National Theatre Live, we broadcast live performances to cinemas around the world. National Theatre: On Demand. In Schools makes acclaimed, curriculum-linked productions free to stream on demand in every primary and secondary school in the country. Online, the NT offers a rich variety of innovative digital content on every aspect of theatre.

We do all we can to keep ticket prices affordable and to reach a wide audience, and use our public funding to maintain artistic risk-taking, accessibility and diversity.

# ₮PUBLIC.

Under the leadership of Artistic Director Oskar Eustis and Executive Director Patrick Willingham, The Public Theater is the only theater in New York City that produces Shakespeare, the classics, musicals, contemporary and experimental pieces in equal measure.

The Public continues the work of its visionary founder, Joe Papp, by acting as an advocate for the theater as an essential cultural force, and leading and framing dialogue on some of the most important issues of our day. Creating theater for one of the largest and most diverse audience bases for nearly 60 years, today the company engages audiences with a breadth of programming that includes, a robust annual season of new musicals and plays at its landmark home at Astor Place; it's beloved Free Shakespeare in the Central Park at the Delacorte Theater; it's Mobile Unit, which tours Shakespearean productions to venues throughout New York's five boroughs; The Public Forum, a series of insightful conversations centered around the themes sparked from the work onstage and around the globe; The Under The Radar Festival, an annual international festival of new work; Public Studio, connecting audiences with artists at the early stage of new work development; Joe's Pub, the best of live music and performance nightly; and Public Works, a major national and international initiative that seeks to engage communities in the creation of participatory theater.

The Public is currently represented on Broadway and around the world by the Tony Award-winning American musical *Hamilton*. The Public is the recipient of 59 Tonys, 168 Obies, 53 Drama Desks, 54 Lortels, 32 OCC Awards and 5 Pulitzer Prizes.

PublicTheater.org

*All The President's Men?,* edited & directed by Nicolas Kent, was originally developed in partnership with The Public Theater.

It was first staged in London on 24th April 2017 at the Vaudeville Theatre, The Strand in a National Theatre & Public Theater co-production.

*(The Vaudeville Theatre was kindly donated for the production by Nimax Theatres)*

# Scene One – Rex Tillerson

From the Senate Foreign Affairs Committee Nomination Hearing of Rex Tillerson for Secretary of State 11th January, 2017

## CHARACTERS

*Panel Members:*
SEN. BOB CORKER, R-TENN., CHAIRMAN
SEN. BENJAMIN L. CARDIN, D-MD., RANKING MEMBER
SEN. MARCO RUBIO, R-FLA.
SEN. ROBERT MENENDEZ, D-N.J.
SEN. RON JOHNSON, R-WIS.
SEN. TIM KAINE, D-VA.
SEN. TODD YOUNG, R-IND.

*Witness:*
REX TILLERSON, NOMINATED TO BE SECRETARY OF STATE

*Protesters:*
FEMALE PROTESTER
MALE PROTESTER

CORKER: The Foreign Relations Committee will come to order.

We appreciate everybody being here as the Senate carries out one of its most important responsibilities, which is to give advice and consent to nominees that are put forth by a President. We would ask those who, like us, have the privilege of being in this room, to respect democracy, to control yourselves in an appropriate manner, and I'm sure that is gonna be the case. This is the best of America here.

Which brings me to you Mr. Tillerson, who by the way, had never met Mr. Trump as I understand until a few weeks ago – a month ago. You've led a global enterprise with 70,000 employees around the world, have been there for forty-one and a half years, have met world leaders, know them up and – up close and personally. To me, that is going to give our new President much greater confidence in your ability to offer advice.

One of your first goals [as Secretary of State] is gonna be is to restore U.S. credibility around the world. You are the person that is charged with being the principal adviser to the President on foreign policy.

So what people here today are gonna want to know is, how are you going to advise him? We know that at the end of the day, you're gonna carry out his policy.

My sense is that you are going to rise to the occasion and that you are going to demonstrate that you are in fact an inspired choice.

Mr. Tillerson, thank you for being here.

TILLERSON: Chairman Corker, Ranking Member Cardin and members of the committee, it's an honor to appear before you today as President-elect Trump's nominee for Secretary of State and seek the approval for my confirmation.

I come before you at a pivotal time in both the history of our nation and our world. And everywhere we look, people in nations are deeply unsettled. We face considerable threats in this evolving new environment.

China has emerged as an economic power in global trade, and our interactions have been both friendly and adversarial. While Russia seeks respect and relevance on the global stage, its recent activities have disregarded America's interest.

Radical Islam is not a new ideology, but it is hateful, deadly and an illegitimate expression of the Islamic faith. Adversaries like Iran and North Korea pose great threats to the world because of their refusal to conform to international norms.

As we confront these realities, how should America respond? My answer is simple; to achieve the stability that is foundational to peace and security, American leadership must not only be renewed, it must be asserted.

In scope of international affairs, America's level of goodwill towards the world is unique and we must continue to display a commitment to personal liberty, human dignity, and principled action in our foreign policy. Quite simply, we are the only global super-power with the means and the moral compass capable of shaping the world for good.

If we do not lead, we risk plunging the world deeper into confusion and danger. But we have stumbled. In recent decades, we have cast American leadership into doubt.

In this campaign, President-elect Trump proposed a bold new commitment to advancing American interest in our foreign policy.

We cannot afford to ignore violations of international accords as we have done with Iran. We cannot continue to accept empty promises, like the ones China has made to pressure North Korea to reform only to shy away from enforcement.

Looking the other way when trust is broken only encourages more bad behavior and it must end. We cannot be accountable though if we are not truthful and honest in our dealings. You are aware [of] my long standing involvement with the Boy Scouts of America. One of our bedrock ideals is honesty. Indeed the phrase "on my honor" begins the Boy Scout oath and it must undergird our foreign policy.

In particular we need to be honest about radical Islam— and the murderous acts committed in its name against Americans and our friends.

The most urgent step in thwarting radical Islam is defeating ISIS.

Russia today poses a danger, but it is not unpredictable in advancing its own interests.

But it was in the absence of American leadership that this door was left open – we sent weak or mixed signals with red lines that turned into green lights.

Our approach to human rights begins by acknowledging that American leadership requires moral clarity.

Our leadership demands utilizing both aid and, where appropriate, economic sanctions as instruments of foreign policy.

I am an engineer by training, I seek to understand the facts, follow where they lead, and apply logic to all international affairs. We must see the world for what it is, have clear priorities, and understand that our power is considerable, but it is not infinite.

If confirmed, I intend to conduct a foreign policy consistent with these ideals. We will never apologize for who we are or what we hold dear.

CORKER:Thank you very much.

With that I'm gonna move to the ranking member, Senator Cardin, and then we'll move to Senator Rubio.

CARDIN: Once again Mr. Tillerson thank you very much.

Do you agree with me that creating stable democratic free societies around the world that support the aspirations of their people including basic human rights, is in our long-term national security interest?

TILLERSON: Without question, Senator.

CARDIN: And do you also agree that Russia, under Mr. Putin's leadership, fails in that category?

TILLERSON: Yes sir.

CARDIN: Does Russia have a – in your view, a legal claim to Crimea?

TILLERSON: No sir, that was a taking of territory that was not theirs.

CARDIN: What would you have done or recommended to have been done to prevent Russia from doing what it did?

TILLERSON: Well, Senator, in terms of the taking of Crimea, my understanding is that that caught a lot of people by surprise. It certainly caught me by surprise, just as a private citizen.

CARDIN: NATO has deployed troops in order to show Russia that Article V means something. I take it you support that type of action?

TILLERSON: Yes, I do. That – that is the type of response that Russia expects. A proportional show of force to indicate to Russia there will be no more taking of territory.

CARDIN: And that's encouraging to me, to hear you say that. Because it's not exactly consistent with what Mr. Trump has been saying in regards to Article V commitments under NATO by the United States.

So let me get to the response that was done. U.S. led sanctions against Russia as a result of its conduct in Ukraine. We went to Europe and were able to get Europe to act. The United States, in my view, wanted to go even further, but we couldn't get Europe to go beyond what they were willing to do. Do you agree or disagree with that strategy for the United States to lead by showing sanctions as we did?

TILLERSON: Senator, sanctions are an important and powerful tool and they're an important tool in terms of deterring additional action. So, yes, American leadership is – is often times, if not almost always, required to demonstrate that first step.

CARDIN: Thank you

CORKER: Senator Rubio

RUBIO: Welcome, Mr. Tillerson.

> Do you believe during the 2016 Presidential campaign, Russian intelligence services directed a campaign of active measures involving the hacking of e-mails, the strategic leak of these e-mails, the use of internet trolls and the dissemination of fake news with the goal of denigrating a Presidential candidate and also undermining faith in our election process?

TILLERSON: Senator, I have had no unclassified briefings because I've not received my clearance yet.

RUBIO: Mr. Tillerson, you've engaged in significant business activities in Russia, so I'm sure you're aware that very few things of a major proportion happen in that country without Vladimir Putin's permission.

> Is it possible for something like this to have happened without Vladimir Putin knowing about it and authorizing it?

TILLERSON: I think that's a fair assumption.

RUBIO: That he would have?

TILLERSON: Yes.

RUBIO: Would you advise the President-elect to repeal the Obama administration's recent executive orders, regarding cybersecurity and Russian interference in the 2016 elections?

TILLERSON: I think the President-elect has indicated and if confirmed, I would support the – what's really required is a comprehensive assessment of our cyber threat and cybersecurity policies.

RUBIO: That is separate from the question of whether people that have already conducted attacks should be sanctioned and singled out.

Do you believe that executive order should be repealed by the incoming President?

TILLERSON: If confirmed Senator, I would want to examine it and all aspects of it.

RUBIO: OK. Let me ask you this question, is Vladimir Putin a war criminal?

TILLERSON: I would not use that term.

RUBIO: Well, let me describe the situation in Aleppo and perhaps that will help you reach that conclusion.

In Aleppo, Mr. Putin has directed his military to conduct a devastating campaign. He's targeted schools, markets – not just assisted the Syrians in doing it – his military has targeted schools and markets and other civilian infrastructure.

It's resulted in the death of thousands of civilians.

So based on all this information and what's publicly in the record about Aleppo and the Russian military, you are still not prepared to say that Vladimir Putin and his military have violated the rules of war and have conducted war crimes in Aleppo?

TILLERSON: Those are very, very serious charges to make and I would want to have much more information before reaching a conclusion. I understand there is a body of record in the public domain, I'm sure there's a body of record in the classified domain. And I think in order to deal with a serious question like this... *(Crosstalk.)*

RUBIO: Mr. Tillerson, what's happened in Aleppo is in the public domain, videos and the pictures are there...

TILLERSON: I would want to be, I would want to be fully informed before advising the President.

RUBIO: There's so much information out there. It should not be hard to say that Vladimir Putin's military has conducted war crimes in Aleppo because it is never acceptable for a military to specifically target civilians, I find it discouraging your inability to cite that, which I think is globally accepted.

I want to, in my last minute and a half here, move really quickly to an additional question. In fact I want to enter into the record, Mr. Chairman without objection.

CORKER: Without objection.

RUBIO: A partial list of political dissidents, journalists and critics of Vladimir Putin who were suspiciously murdered or died under highly suspicious circumstances.

Mr. Tillerson, do you believe that Vladimir Putin and his cronies are responsible for ordering the murder of countless dissidents, journalists and political opponents?

TILLERSON: I do not have sufficient information to make that claim.

RUBIO: Are you aware that people who oppose Vladimir Putin wind up dead all over the world, poisoned, shot in the back of the head? And do you think that was coincidental or do you think that it is quite possible or likely as I believe, that they were part of an effort to murder his political opponents?

TILLERSON: Well, people who speak up for freedom in regimes that are oppressive are often at threat and these things happen to them. In terms of assigning specific responsibilities, I would have to have more information.

I look forward, if confirmed, to becoming fully informed. But I am not willing to make conclusions on what is only publicly available or had been publicly…

RUBIO: None of this is classified, Mr. Tillerson, these people are dead. Political opponents…

TILLERSON: Your question was – your question was [about] people who were directly responsible for that. I'm not disputing these people are dead.

CORKER: Senator Menendez.

MENENDEZ: Thank you.

Mr. Tillerson, congratulations on your nomination.

I assume to some degree, that you've had some discussion [with President-elect Trump] about what it is that that world view is going to be in order to understand whether you're willing to execute that on behalf of the person you're gonna work for.

TILLERSON: In a broad construct and in terms of the principles that are going to guide that, yes, sir.

MENENDEZ: And I would have thought that Russia would be at the very top of that considering all the actions that have taken place. Is – did that not happen?

TILLERSON: That has not occurred yet, Senator.

MENENDEZ: That's pretty amazing.

You built a career on ExxonMobil that you said afforded you the opportunity to engage regularly with world leaders, including Vladimir Putin in Russia.

In 2013, he awarded you with the Order of Friendship Award and you had direct and personal access to the Russian President over the course of your tenure there.

In 2014, ExxonMobil lobbied aggressively against sanctions on Russia after their invasion of Ukraine.

You employed well-known Washington-based lobbyists who support these efforts. You personally visited the White House and reported that you were engaged quote, "at the highest levels of government." In essence, Exxon became the in-house lobbyist for Russia against these sanctions.

Sanctions are one of the most effective diplomatic tools in our arsenal.

Now, today, in response to the previous question by Senator Cardin, you said sanctions are a powerful tool.

But you have made statements and given speeches where you have said you do not believe sanctions are a useful tool.

So if sanctions are not a useful tool, have you changed your view? What are the tools of peaceful diplomacy you will use? What are you gonna say to Vladimir Putin when he says to you, but Rex, you said sanctions were bad?

TILLERSON: Senator, I think it's important to acknowledge that when sanctions are imposed, they by their design are going to harm American business. That's the idea, it's to disrupt America's business engagement in whatever country's being targeted for sanctions. And so broadly...

MENENDEZ: I don't think it's to disrupt American business. I think it's to disrupt the economies of those countries.

TILLERSON: The intent behind the sanctions is to disrupt that country's access to American business, investment, money flows, technology... *(Crosstalk)*

MENENDEZ: ... the financial sectors?

TILLERSON: Correct. The fact is, sanctions in order to be implemented, do impact American business interests.

In protecting America's interest, sanctions are a powerful tool. Let's design them well, let's target them well and then, let's enforce them fully...

MENENDEZ: In your opening statement, you said "We are the only global super power with the means and moral compass capable of shaping the world for good."

Mr. Tillerson, our efforts in leading the international community for example, in sanctions against our adversaries like Iran and North Korea, represent exactly that.

Leadership and a moral compass, it's not about disadvantaging American businesses. It's about putting patriotism over profit.

Now, you lobbied against the Comprehensive Iran Sanctions Act. [When] you were the head of ExxonMobil, you wanted to eliminate secondary sanctions that would prevent joint ventures.

This makes sense as in 2003, 2004 and 2005, you were engaged to a subsidiary company in businesses with countries who the United States listed as state sponsors of terrorism. Countries that, except for the maneuver of your subsidiary, ExxonMobil could not have been dealing with.

So my question is, with that as a history, [in] 2011 when you oversaw an ExxonMobil deal with the Kurdish Regional Government in Iraq after the United States government expressly did not want to see that happen – fearing that a deal would undermine the U.S. policy of one Iraq and lead the country closer to civil war – what message are you now going to be able to send to American business who are intent on pursuing their own interests at the expense of U.S. policies and political stability in foreign countries?

TILLERSON: Well, there was a lot in that question, Senator…

MENENDEZ: I'll give you the rest of my time *(inaudible)*.

TILLERSON: … around which I could respond. First, I have never lobbied against sanctions personally. I continue to believe sanctions…

MENENDEZ: But the company that you directed did.

TILLERSON: To – to my knowledge, Exxon never directly lobbied against sanctions. Not to my knowledge.

In terms of all the other actions that were mentioned there – they were all undertaken with a great deal of transparency and openness and engagement and input to the process.

CORKER: Senator Johnson.

JOHNSON: Thank you, Mr. Chairman.

You said that Russia is not unpredictable. "Russia does not think like we do." Can you further expand on both of those comments?

TILLERSON: Well, in terms of their...

PROTESTER: Why does Tillerson [friendzies] Putin – because they both want to drill and burn the Arctic! That will ruin the climate and destroy the future for our children and grandchildren. Please don't put Exxon in charge of the State Department.

JOHNSON: If you forgot the question, it was – it was explain your comments that Russia is predictable, basically and that Russia does not think like we do?

TILLERSON: Well, in my experience– the time I've spent in Russia as an observer, my experience with the Russians are that they are very calculating and they're very strategic in their thinking and they develop a plan.

PROTESTER: You have treated the world's most vulnerable communities as expendable. In our home state of Texas people are resisting out-dated pipelines. Oil is dead. Senators, be brave, stop this man. Protect the vulnerable.

CORKER: Mr. Tillerson. Now you can maybe answer the question unimpeded.

TILLERSON: Well, Russia, more than anything wants to re-establish its role in the global world order. They believe they deserve a rightful role because they are a nuclear power.

And so the steps being taken [now] are simply to make that point that Russia is here.

I think the important conversation that we have to have with them is – does Russia want to now and forever be an adversary of the United States or does Russia desire a different relationship?

CORKER: Thank you, sir.

Senator Kaine?

KAINE: Mr. Tillerson, thank you for your willingness to serve.

How much information do you have about financial connections between President-elect Trump, the Trump family or Trump organizations and Russian individuals or organizations or the Russian government?

TILLERSON: I have no knowledge.

KAINE: And if I asked you the same question and I substituted Turkey, China, Pakistan or Japan for Russia in that question, would your answer be the same?

TILLERSON: I have no knowledge.

KAINE: So I gather from your answer that you'll then have no way of knowing how actions proposed by a President Trump, regarding those countries or others, would effect his personal or family financial interests?

TILLERSON: I have no knowledge.

KAINE: How is a Congress of the American public supposed to fully judge the actions, official actions, proposed by a President Trump, if we lack basic information about how those actions may benefit his personal finances?

TILLERSON: That's a question that others will have to address, Senator.

KAINE: You're aware that government leaders of many of the countries that you dealt with in your capacity as CEO of ExxonMobil have used their positions of leadership to greatly advance their personal wealth while they were in office, correct?

TILLERSON: I have no direct knowledge of that.

KAINE: But you've read press accounts, for example, about folks like Vladimir Putin or the leaders of Equatorial Guinea and other nations suggesting that they have amassed great personal wealth while in office, correct?

TILLERSON: I'm aware of the press reports.

KAINE: Do you think that such behavior by a head of government is in accord with values of the United States or contrary to U.S. values?

TILLERSON: If the reports are true, and there has been inappropriate taking of funds that belong to the – rightfully to the government and if that is not provided for under the government's laws, then that would be contrary to our values which are to respect the laws.

KAINE: I wanna switch and ask you some questions about climate.

InsideClimate News did an eight month investigation, and produced a nine-part series that was a finalist for the Pulitzer Prize, all on the question of ExxonMobil's knowledge of basic climate science.

These articles conclude the following:

1. ExxonMobil concluded as early as the 1970s that pollution from $CO_2$ released by the burning fossil fuels, was affecting the climate in potentially destructive ways.

2. Despite this knowledge, ExxonMobil took public positions against the scientific position regarding climate science.

3. ExxonMobil funded outside organizations that publicly downplayed and obscured the scientific consensus.

And

4. ExxonMobil despite claims to the contrary, continues to provide funding, if at a lower level, to outside groups that deny, downplay or obscure this scientific consensus.

Are these conclusions about ExxonMobil's history of promoting and funding climate science denial, despite its internal awareness of the reality of climate change, during your tenure with the company, true or false?

TILLERSON: Senator, since I'm no longer with ExxonMobil, I'm in no position to speak on their behalf. The question would have to be put to them.

KAINE: I'm not asking you to speak on ExxonMobil's behalf. You were with the company for nearly forty-two years?

TILLERSON: That is correct.

KAINE: And for the majority of your time you were with the company in an executive and management position?

TILLERSON: Approximately half the time.

KAINE: And you became CEO in 2006?

TILLERSON: Correct.

KAINE: So I'm not asking you on behalf of ExxonMobil; you resigned from ExxonMobil. I'm asking you whether those allegations are true or false.

TILLERSON: The question would have to be put to ExxonMobil.

KAINE: Do you lack the knowledge to answer my question or are you refusing to answer my question?

TILLERSON: A little of both.

KAINE: I – I have a hard time believing you lack the knowledge to answer my question, but that's an editorial comment just like your comment was an editorial comment.

CORKER: Senator Young.

YOUNG: As the nation's chief diplomat, it's really important [to] speak with a voice that is perceived to be the voice of the President of the United States. There cannot be space between the policies you are putting forward and those that are embraced by our now President-elect.

He has a history of utilizing social media, Twitter in particular. And some of the President-elect tweets appear to be quickly drafted. So, this gives some concern you might not be empowered to actually serve as the chief diplomat. You would lack credibility. How would you ensure that the legs are not cut out from underneath you as the nation's chief diplomat?

TILLERSON: I don't think I'm going to be telling the boss how he ought to communicate with the American people. That's going to be his choice. But in carrying out the foreign policy, including traveling abroad I understand your point. I'm overseas and that – it would be my expectation that any way the President might choose to communicate – through whatever method, would be supportive of that policy we both agreed on.

YOUNG: So do you have in mind any contingency plans to …

TILLERSON: Yes, I have his …

YOUNG: to address …

TILLERSON: I have his cell phone number.

YOUNG: OK.

TILLERSON: And he's promised me he'll answer.

CORKER: – and he does. I'll turn to Senator Cardin.

CARDIN: Thank you, Mr. Chairman. In response to Senator Menendez's questions about lobbying I'm going to ask consent to put into the record the lobbying disclosure form from ExxonMobil Corporation that indicates that approximately $3.4 million was spent in lobbying on behalf of the Iran Sanctions Act.

Put that into the record, Mr. Chairman?

*He hands the document to CORKER who has left his seat to talk to someone behind him. CARDIN goes to place it on CORKER's desk and then decides to place it to his left.*

Without objection.

*He laughs.*

I wanted to be chairman.

*Laughter. CORKER returns.*

*(To CORKER.)* … putting some information for the record.

CORKER: I understand you became chairman while I was talking.

*Laughter.*

But…

CARDIN: You've got to watch it. You've always got to watch out.

CORKER: Without objection.

CARDIN: Thank you.

I'll turn to Senator Rubio.

RUBIO: Do you believe China is one of the world's worst human rights violators?

TILLERSON: China has serious human rights violations. Relative to categorizing it against other nations, I would have to have more information, but they certainly have serious human rights violations.

RUBIO: OK. Since President Rodrigo Duterte took office last June, the Los Angeles Times reports that roughly over 6,200 people have been killed in the Philippines by police and vigilantes in alleged drug raids. In your view, is this the right way to conduct an anti-drug campaign?

TILLERSON: Senator, the U.S. and the people of the Philippines have a long-standing friendship. I think it's important that we keep that in perspective, in engaging with the government of the Philippines.

RUBIO: That's correct, Mr. Tillerson. But my question is about the 6,200 people killed in these alleged drug raids. Do you believe that that is an appropriate way to conduct that operation?

TILLERSON: Senator, if confirmed, again, it's an area that I'd want to understand in greater detail in terms of the facts on the ground. I'm not disputing anything you're saying because I know you have access to information that I do not have.

RUBIO: This is from the Los Angeles Times.

TILLERSON: Well, again, I'm not going to rely on solely what I read in the newspapers. I will go to the facts on the ground. I'm sure there's good credible information available through our various government agencies.

RUBIO: Well, one of the sources is President Duterte himself, who openly brags about the people that are being shot and killed on the streets, who he has determined are drug dealers without any trial. So, if in fact he continues to brag about it, would that be reliable information that you would look at and say, OK, it's happening?

TILLERSON: If the facts – if the facts are in fact supportive of those numbers and those actions, then I don't think any of us would accept that as a proper way to deal with offenders, no matter how egregious.

RUBIO: I'm sure you're also aware of the lack of both religious freedoms and the lack of rights of women in Saudi Arabia. In your opinion, is Saudi Arabia a human rights violator?

TILLERSON: Saudi Arabia certainly does not share the same values of America. However, American interests have been advocating in Saudi Arabia for some time. And I think the question is what is the pace of progress that should be expected for the Kingdom of Saudi Arabia to advance rights to women and others in the country.

RUBIO: And as it currently stands, do you consider what they're doing, to be human rights violations?

TILLERSON: I would need to have greater information, Senator, in order to make a true determination of that.

RUBIO: You're not familiar with the state of affairs for people in Saudi Arabia? What life is like for women? They can't drive. They have people jailed and lashed. You are familiar with all of that?

TILLERSON: Yes, Senator, I'm familiar with all of that. And…

RUBIO: So what more information would you need?

TILLERSON: I share all the same values that you share, and want the same things for people the world over in terms of freedoms.

But I'm also clear-eyed and realistic about dealing in cultures. These are centuries-long cultural differences. It doesn't mean that we can't affect them and affect them to change.

CORKER: Thank you. Senator Menendez?

MENENDEZ: Thank you, Mr. Chairman.

You stated, on the record, that neither you nor Exxon ever lobbied against sanctions; that you were merely seeking information.

I have four different lobbying reports totaling millions of dollars, as required by the Lobbying Disclosure Act, that lists ExxonMobil's lobbying activities on four specific pieces of legislation authorizing sanctions.

When you employ lobbyists, who submit lobbying forms under the law, you are taking a position. Is that not correct?

TILLERSON: I haven't seen the form you're holding in your hand, so I don't know whether it indicates were we lobbying for the sanctions or were we lobbying against the sanctions.

MENENDEZ: I know you weren't lobbying for the sanctions, but…

TILLERSON: Well, if the form there…

MENENDEZ: It says, for example, here, specific lobbying issues: Russian Aggression Prevention of 2014, provisions related to energy. You weren't lobbying *for* sanctions on energy, were you?

TILLERSON: I think that's a description of the subject that was discussed. And I haven't seen the form, Senator, so I don't want to be presumptuous here.

MENENDEZ: You don't need a lobbying disclosure form to simply seek information and clarification about a bill. That's not lobbying. Lobbying specifically is to promote a view, a position.

I'd ask unanimous consent to have these included in the record.

CORKER: Without objection.

MENENDEZ: OK. All right.

Last week, the President-elect tweeted that any money spent on building the great wall will be paid by Mexico.

I also want to point out the last time a country tried to wall itself completely from its neighbor was in Berlin in 1961 and that wall was constructed by communist East Germany.

Former Mexican President last week tweeted and it seems that's how we're conducting foreign policy, by tweets these days, that "Trump may ask whoever he wants but still neither myself nor Mexico are going to pay for his racist monument, another promise he can't keep," close quotes. The President-elect has repeatedly referred to Mexican citizens who have come to the United States as quote "people that have lots of problems. They're bringing drugs, they're bringing crime, they're rapists and some I assume are good people." So Mr. Tillerson, do you think Mexicans are criminals, drug dealers and rapists?

TILLERSON: I would never characterize an entire population with any single term at all.

MENENDEZ: Do you think that those comments help our relationship with Mexico, our third largest trading partner, [our] second largest goods export market?

TILLERSON: Mexico is a long-standing neighbor and friend of this country.

MENENDEZ: Mr. Tillerson, between 2003 and 2005, ExxonMobil sold $53 million worth of chemicals and fuel additives to Iranian customers. Alarmingly, Exxon did not originally disclose this business with Iran in its annual report with the S.E.C. ExxonMobil only disclosed this information after receiving a letter from the S.E.C asking for explanations because Iran at the time, was, "subject to export controls imposed on Iran as a result of its actions in support of terrorism, and in pursuit of weapons of mass destruction and missile programs." It went on to say, "We know that your form 10k does not contain any disclosure about your operations in Iran, Syria and Sudan."

Exxon's response has been that the transactions were legal because the chemicals' joint venture with Shell was based in Europe and the transactions did not involve any U.S. employees. In other words, this would clearly seem as a move designed to do business with Iran to evade sanctions on Iran.

One of the customers was the Iranian National Oil Company, which is wholly-owned by the Iranian government [and] is an agent or affiliate of Iran's Islamic Revolutionary Guard Corps.

They are currently in Syria right now helping Assad remain in power. So, can you tell the committee whether these business dealings with Iran did not fund any state sponsored terrorism activities by Iran?

TILLERSON: Senator, as I indicated earlier, I do not recall the details of the circumstances around what you just described. The question would have to go to ExxonMobil for them to be able to answer that. I –

MENENDEZ: You have no recollection of this as the CEO?

TILLERSON: I don't – I don't recall all the details around it, no, sir.

MENENDEZ: It wouldn't come to your level? It wouldn't come to your level that the securities and exchange commission raised questions with your company about lack of disclosure?

TILLERSON: 2006 would have been the first year that I would have been looking at those things. I just don't recall this.

MENENDEZ: Do you recall whether ExxonMobil was doing business with three different state sponsors of terrorism, including Iran in the first place?

TILLERSON: No, I don't recall that. Again, I'd have to look back and refresh myself.

MENENDEZ: I – I would hope that you would do so. And, I would be willing to hear your response for the record. Because, I think it's important.

I have one final question, Mr. Chairman. In essence my big question for you. It's an article that appeared in Time Magazine, and, I really want to hear your honest response to this.

And, I'm going to quote from the article. It says, what the Russians want from Tillerson is bigger than sanctions relief. They want to see a whole new approach to American diplomacy. One that stops putting principles ahead of profits. Focusing instead on getting the best political bargain available. And treats Russia as an equal.

"For the next four years, we can forget about America as the bearer of values," said a former Russian Energy Minister who went to join the opposition. "America's going to play the deal game under Trump. And, for Putin, that's a very comfortable environment."

"It's an environment where statesmen sit before a map of the world and they haggle over pieces available to them."

"Through the canny eyes of the political dealmaker, many of Washington's oldest commitments in Europe and the Middle East could come to be seen much the same way, as a stack of bargaining chips to be traded rather than principles to be upheld."

That's not you being quoted but, that's a characterization, it's a characterization I've heard many times. I want to give you an open opportunity to respond to it.

TILLERSON: Well, I haven't seen the article in its entirety. But, I'll just deal with the quotes that you read. If you conclude that that's the characterization of me, then, I have really done a poor job today. Because, what I've hoped to do in today's exchange on the questions is to demonstrate to you that I'm a very open and transparent person.

I do have strong values that are grounded in – in my American ideals and beliefs, the values I was raised with. I've spoken to the Boy Scouts this morning earlier, they're underpinned by those same values, duty to God and country, duty to others and duty to yourself and that has guided my life for all of my life. And, it will guide my values and it will guide the way in which I will represent the American people if given the chance to do so.

I understand full well the responsibilities and seriousness of it. I don't view this as a game in any way, as that article seems to imply. So, I hope if I've done nothing else today, you at least know me better.

*Blackout. End of scene.*

## SCENE TWO – TOM PRICE

From the Senate Health, Education, Labor and Pensions
Committee Nomination Hearing of Dr Tom Price for
Secretary U.S. Department of Health & Human Services
January 18, 2017

CHARACTERS

*Panel Members:*
SEN. LAMAR ALEXANDER, R-TENN. CHAIRMAN
SEN. PATTY MURRAY, D-WASH. RANKING
MEMBER
SEN. BERNARD SANDERS, I-VT.
SEN. ORRIN G. HATCH, R-UTAH
SEN. AL FRANKEN, D-MINN.
SEN. MICHAEL BENNET, D-COLO.
SEN. CHRISTOPHER S. MURPHY, D-CONN.
SEN. ELIZABETH WARREN, D-MASS.

*Witness:*
REP. TOM PRICE, R-GA., NOMINATED TO
BE SECRETARY OF HEALTH AND HUMAN
SERVICES

ALEXANDER: The Committee on Health, Education, Labor
and Pensions will come to order.

Today, we're reviewing the nomination of Dr. Tom Price to
be the secretary of health and human services.

This is a courtesy hearing. Dr. Price will be before the
Finance Committee next Tuesday. We don't vote on his
nomination. They vote on his nomination and will be
the ones that report it to the floor of the Senate. We have
the hearing because we have some of the health care
jurisdiction, we would like to talk to him about especially
those issues.

Dr. Price, if you're confirmed to lead the Department of Health and Human Services, you'll be running an organization that spends $1.1 trillion a year.

You'll be overseeing Medicare and Medicaid, mental and substance abuse programs and one of the first responsibilities that you will have is to give us your advice, about how to repair the damage that the Affordable Care Act has caused to so many Americans and how to replace it or to replace parts of it with concrete practical alternatives that give Americans more choices of lower cost insurance.

President-elect Trump said on 60 Minutes that replacement and repeal of Obamacare would be done "simultaneously" – his word.

To me, that means at the same time.

The American people deserve health care reform that's done in the right way, for the right reasons and the right amount of time. It's not about developing a quick fix. It's about working toward long-term solutions that work for everyone.

But I do look forward to hearing from you, how you suggest we approach this.

Senator Murray?

MURRAY: Thank you very much, Chairman Alexander.

Congressman Price, I have serious concerns about your qualifications and plans for the department you hope to lead.

Just last week, you voted to begin the process of ripping apart our health care system without any plan to replace it, even though more and more members of your own party are expressing serious doubts about its ability to unify around a plan and knowing that in a matter of weeks, you could be leading the department whose core responsibility is to enhance America's health and well-being.

So I will be very interested in hearing your explanation of how we would keep the promises your party has made to the American people about their health care.

Medicare is another issue. President-elect Trump campaigned on promises to protect Medicare and Medicaid. You have said you plan to overhaul Medicare in the first six to eight months of this administration in a way that would end the guarantee of full coverage, that so many seniors and people with disabilities rely on.

You have put forward policies that would shift a trillion dollars in Medicaid costs to our states, squeezing their budgets and taking coverage away from struggling children and workers and families. And while President-elect Trump has said that Medicare should be able to negotiate lower drug prices for seniors, you have repeatedly opposed efforts to do that.

Finally, Congressman Price, the Office of Congressional Ethics has now been asked to investigate serious concerns and questions about your medical stock trades during your time in the House. I and other Democrats have repeatedly called for hearings on your nomination to be delayed until such an investigation is complete. It is disappointing to us that instead, Republicans are moving forward with your nomination before we have all the facts. I hope you've come prepared to be fully transparent with us in your explanation.

Thank you, Mr. Chairman.

ALEXANDER: Thank you, Senator Murray.

Dr. Price, welcome to the committee.

PRICE: Thank you, Mr. Chairman.

I want to thank you all for the opportunity to speak with you today and engage in the discussion about the road ahead for our great nation.

We all come to public service in our own unique ways that inform who we are and why we serve. My experience as a physician and later as a legislator has provided a holistic view of the complex interactions that take place every day across our communities.

In Congress, I've been fortunate as well to be part of collaborations that broke through party lines to solve problems. Just this past Congress, it was a bi-partisan effort that succeeded in ridding Medicare of a broken physician payment system, and which has now begun the creation of a new system, which will help ensure that seniors have better access to higher quality care.

So if confirmed, my obligation will be to carry to the Department of Health and Human Services both an appreciation for bipartisan, team-driven policy-making, and a lifetime commitment to improving the health and well-being of the American people.

ALEXANDER: Thank you, Dr. Price. Senator Murray?

MURRAY: Thank you, Mr. Chairman.

Congressman Price, recent press reports about your investments in the Australian biotech company Innate Immunotherapeutics, a company working to develop new drugs, on four separate occasions between January 2015 and August 2016. You made the decision to purchase that stock, not a broker, yes or no?

PRICE: That was a decision that I made, yes.

MURRAY: You were offered an opportunity to purchase stock at a lower price than was available to the general public, yes or no?

PRICE: The initial purchase in January of 2015 was at the market price. The secondary purchase in June through August, September of 2016 was at a price that was available to individuals who were participating in a private placement offering.

MURRAY: It was lower than was available to the general public, correct?

PRICE: I don't know that it was. It was – the same price that everybody paid for the private placement offering.

MURRAY: Well, Congressman Chris Collins who sits on President-elect Trump's transition team, is both an investor and a board member of the company. He was reportedly overheard just last week off the House floor bragging about how he had made people millionaires from a stock tip.

Congressman Price, in our meeting, you informed me that you made these purchases based on conversations with Representative Collins. Is that correct?

PRICE: No. What I…

MURRAY: That is what you said to me in my office.

PRICE: What I believe I said to you was that I learned of the company from Congressman Collins.

MURRAY: Did Representative Collins tell you anything that could be considered quote, "a stock tip", yes or no?

PRICE: I don't believe so, no.

MURRAY: Well if – if you're telling me he gave you information about a company, you were offered shares in the company at prices not available to the public, you bought those shares. Is that not a stock tip?

PRICE: That's not what happened. What happened was that he mentioned, he – he talked about the company and the work that they were doing in trying to solve the challenge of progressive secondary multiple sclerosis, which is a very debilitating disease and one that I…

MURRAY: I'm well aware of that, but…

PRICE: … had the opportunity to treat patients when I was in practice.

MURRAY: I'm aware of...

PRICE: I studied the company for a period of time and felt that it had some significant merit and purchased the initial shares on the stock exchange itself.

MURRAY: Congressman Price, I have very limited time. Let me go on.

Your purchases occurred while the 21st Century Cures Act, which had several provisions that could impact drug developers like Innate Immunotherapeutics was being negotiated, and again, just days before you were notified to prepare for a final vote on the bill. Congressman, do you believe it is appropriate for a senior member of Congress actively involved in policy making in the health sector to repeatedly personally invest in a drug company that could benefit from those actions, yes or no?

PRICE: Well, that's not what happened.

MURRAY: Well, let me just say that I believe it's inappropriate and we need answers to this regarding whether you and Congressman Collins used your access to non-public information when you bought at prices that were unavailable to the public.

PRICE: I had no access to non-public information.

MURRAY: Well, we – we will go on.

Just days ago, President-elect Trump said his plan would provide insurance for everybody. Do you share those goals?

PRICE: I think it's absolutely imperative that we – have a system in place that has patients at the center and allows for every single American to have the opportunity to gain access to the kind of coverage...

MURRAY: You share his goal of insurance for everybody?

PRICE: That's been always my stated goal.

MURRAY: OK. If your repeal plan, the Empowering Patients First Act, was signed into law, would you consider these commitments to insure all Americans and leave no one worse off be met?

PRICE: My role in – in Congress was to always make certain that individuals have the opportunity to gain access to the kind of coverage that they desired and that they had the financial feasibility to do so.

MURRAY: Your bill only allows people with pre-existing conditions to obtain health insurance if they maintained continuous insurance for eighteen months prior.

Under your plan, insurance companies could deny those Americans coverage for pre-existing conditions, yes or no, under your bill?

PRICE: It's a broader question than that because we would put in place high risk pools and individual health pools that would allow every single person in the individual small group market who are the ones challenged with pre-existing illness to be able to gain access, again, to the coverage that they want.

MURRAY: Well, I think we disagree on the consequences of that. Your bill would also repeal dependent coverage available to young adults up to age twenty-six, that is correct, right?

PRICE: The bill that I authored did not include coverage up to age twenty-six. The insurance companies have said that they were working that in their plans going forward.

MURRAY: OK. And your bill takes away current benefits, which include prescription drugs, mental health and substance use disorder benefits and maternity coverage among others. That is correct, right?

PRICE: There are other factors that we would put in place that would make certain that individuals have the care and the kind of coverage that they needed for whatever diagnoses would befall them.

MURRAY: Again, I disagree with the consequences, but your bill didn't cover that.

Your bill also repeals the lifetime limits on coverage that helps a lot of people who are sick and have high medical expenses, like a person with cancer, yes or no?

PRICE: Again, it's a larger question because what we would put is a different construct in place that would allow for every single person to gain access to the coverage that they want and have nobody fall through the cracks.

ALEXANDER: Thank you, Senator Murray.

Senator Sanders?

SANDERS: Thank you, Mr. Chairman.

Congressman, during the course of his campaign, Mr. Trump said over and over again that he would not cut Social Security; not cut Medicare; not cut Medicaid. Let me read some quotes.

*(A tweet is displayed.)*

On May 7th, 2015, Mr. Trump tweeted, "I was the first and only potential GOP candidate to state there will be no cuts to Social Security, Medicare and Medicaid." On April 18th, 2015, he said, quote, "Every Republican wants to do a big number on Social Security. They want to do it on Medicare. They want to do it on Medicaid. And we can't do that and it's not fair to the people that have been paying in for years" end of quote.

March 29th, 2016, Trump said, "You know, Paul Ryan wants to knock out Social Security, knock it down, way down. He wants to knock Medicare way down. They want to really cut, and they want to cut it very substantially – the Republicans – and I'm not going to do that."

On and on and on. Point being, this is not something he said in passing. I think it is likely he won the election because millions of working-class people and senior citizens heard him say he was not going to cut Social Security, Medicare and Medicaid.

Congressman Price, a very simple question: Is the President-elect, Mr. Trump, going to keep his word to the American people and not cut Social Security, Medicare and Medicaid? Or did he lie to the American people?

PRICE: I haven't had extensive discussions with him about the comments that he made, but I have no reasons to believe that he's changed his position.

SANDERS: So you are telling us that to the best of your knowledge, Mr. Trump will not cut Social Security, Medicare and Medicaid?

PRICE: As I say, I have no reason to believe that that position has changed.

SANDERS: Quoting Mr. Trump again, or at least paraphrasing him, just last week he said, roughly speaking, pharma is getting away with murder. Do you recall that tweet?

PRICE: I do.

SANDERS: OK. There are many of us on this side of the aisle who are working on legislation that would end the absurdity of the American people being ripped off by the pharmaceutical industry, who two years ago made – the top five companies made $50 billion in profits, while one out of five Americans can't afford to fill the prescriptions their doctors write.

Will you and will the President-elect join us in legislation we are working on which, number one, will allow Medicare to negotiate prices with the drug companies and lower prices; and number two, allow the American people to bring in less expensive medicine from Canada and other countries?

PRICE: The issue of drug pricing and drug costs is one of great concern to all Americans.

SANDERS: But you are aware, sir – I don't mean to interrupt – we don't have a lot of time. We are paying by far the highest prices in the world for prescription drugs?

PRICE: I think that's the case. I'd have to look at the statistics. I think there are a lot of reasons for that. And if we get to the root cause of what that is, then I think we can actually solve it with bipartisan... *(crosstalk)*

SANDERS: Well, one of the root causes is that every other major country on earth negotiates drug prices with the pharmaceutical industry. In our country, the drug companies can double their prices. There is no law to prevent them from doing that.

Will you work with us so that Medicare negotiates prices with the pharmaceutical industry?

PRICE: You have my commitment to work with you and others to make certain that the drug pricing is reasonable and that individuals across this land have access to the medications that they need.

SANDERS: That wasn't quite the answer to the question that I asked.

Congressman Price, the United States of America is the only major country on earth that does not guarantee health care to all people as a right. Canada does it. Every major country in Europe does it. Do you believe that health care is a right of all Americans whether they're rich or they're poor?

PRICE: Yes. We're a compassionate society.

SANDERS: No, we are not a compassionate society. In terms of our relationship to poor and working people, our record is worse than virtually any other country on earth. We have the highest rate of childhood poverty of any other major country on earth. And half of our older workers have nothing set aside for retirement.

So I don't think compared to other countries, we are particularly compassionate. But my question is in other countries, all people have the right to get health care. Do you believe we should move in that direction?

PRICE: I look forward to working with you to make certain that every single American has access to the highest quality care and coverage that is possible.

SANDERS: "Has access to" does not mean that they are guaranteed health care. I have access to buying a $10 million home. I don't have the money to do that.

ALEXANDER: Thank you, Senator Sanders. Senator Hatch?

HATCH: Thank you, Mr. Chairman.

Welcome to the committee. Having worked with you over the years, I've found you to be always very, very knowledgeable.

PRICE: Thank you.

HATCH: Very up front and very straightforward, very honest, and somebody who really understands the health care system of this country.

[Congressman Price] you're just perfectly situated to be able to help turn it around and get it so it works.

Now, Dr. Price, some of my colleagues have criticized you for your health-related stock holdings while serving in the House. Now, not only do House rules not prohibit members from trading stocks, but it is also not an uncommon practice for members of Congress.

This appears to be nothing more than a hypocritical attack on your good character. And I personally resent it because you have always disclosed. Can you confirm that you have always followed the law relating to trading in stocks while serving as a member of Congress?

PRICE: Thank you, Sir. Everything that we have done has been above-board, transparent, ethical and legal.

HATCH: I take it that you believe that getting health care closer to the people is a far better thing than everybody pontificating from Washington, D.C.?

PRICE: I think the more involvement that patients and families and doctors can have in medical decisions, the higher quality care we'll have.

HATCH: Well, thank you sir. I think you're a great nomination.

PRICE: Thank you.

ALEXANDER: Thank you, Senator Hatch. Senator Franken?

FRANKEN: Dr. Price, it was nice meeting you the other day.

PRICE: Yeah, it was good.

FRANKEN: Did you enjoy meeting me?

PRICE: Thank you. I did, I did.

*(Laughter.)*

I enjoyed our discussion about our gray hair.

FRANKEN: Dr. Price between 1993 and 2012, you were a shareholder of big tobacco companies, meaning that you personally benefited from tobacco sales. Meanwhile, you voted against landmark legislation in 2009 that gave the FDA the authority to regulate tobacco.

Congressman Price, you're a physician, which means you took the Hippocratic oath, a pledge to do no harm. How do you square reaping personal financial gain from the sales of an addictive product that kills millions of Americans every decade with also voting against measures to reduce the death toll inflicted by tobacco?

PRICE: I have no idea what stocks I held in the 90s or the 2000s or even now.

FRANKEN: You know, I find it very hard to believe that you did not know that you had tobacco stocks.

We talked a little bit about the Zimmer Biomet. Your broker bought it on March 17, 2016. You did introduce a bill a week later on March 23, 2016. You say that you did not know then that you had this stock. It was to delay a federal rule that would have reduced the profitability of the company's joint [*inaudible*] – to delay a rule that would hurt the company.

I think our job in this body and in Congress and in government is to avoid the appearance of conflict. And boy, you have not done this.

Your latest plan, Empowering Patients First Act is detailed in this article from the New England Journal of Medicine. It's called, "Care for the Vulnerable vs. Cash for the Powerful – Trump's Pick for HHS."

I'll just read a random paragraph. "Price's record demonstrates less concern for the sick, the poor and the health of the public and much greater concern for the economic well-being of their physician care-givers." What your plan does is it gives a tax credit to Americans to buy health insurance. It's no different for someone who's poor, someone who makes $20,000, $30,000 and to Bill Gates.

It is an incredibly regressive system.

ALEXANDER: Senator Bennet?

BENNET: Thank you, Mr. Chairman and I should tell you that I have never shown my knee to any nominee before Dr. Price came to my office, but he gave me some free medical advice and I'm grateful for that.

*(Laughter.)*

PRICE: How you doing?

BENNET: Free health care – I'm terrible, it's terrible but I'll talk to you after it's over.

*(Laughter.)*

It's not because of you…

PRICE: I can't ask you but I'm curious as to whether or not you've gotten the MRI?

BENNET: Today, 10 o'clock.

PRICE: Today? Good. *(Crosstalk)*

BENNET: Congressman, I know you've been chair of the House Budget Committee. I know you're a member of the Tea Party, [and have] been a strong advocate of introducing a Balanced Budget for a Stronger America.

The first order of business for the Republican majority here has been to pass a budget resolution repealing the A[ffordable] C[are] A[ct]. And this budget resolution specifically authorizes $9 trillion in additional debt over the next ten years.

And let me read – my colleague, a smart guy who's here, Senator Paul, highlighted in his floor speech on January 4th. He said quote, "The more things change, the more they seem to stay the same. Republicans won the White House, Republicans control the Senate, Republicans control the House. And what will be the first order of business for the new Republican majority? To pass a budget that never balances. To pass a budget that will add $9.7 trillion of new debt over ten years."

"Ten trillion dollars worth of new debt. I'm not for it," said that honest man.

So I ask you, sir, are you aware that behind closed doors, Republican leadership wrote into this bill that any replacement to the Affordable Care Act would be exempt from Senate rules that prohibit large increases to the deficit?

PRICE: As you may know, Senator, I stepped aside as chairman of the Budget Committee at the beginning of this year, so I wasn't involved in the writing of…

BENNET: You have been the Budget Committee chairman. You are a member of the Tea Party Caucus. You have said over and over again, that the reason you've come to Washington is to reduce our debt. I assume you are very well aware of the vehicle that is being used to repeal the Affordable Care Act. Do you support a budget that increases the debt by $10 trillion dollars?

PRICE: What I support is an opportunity to use the reconciliation to address the real challenges in the Affordable Care Act and to make certain that we put in place —a provision that allows us to move the health care system in a much better direction.

ALEXANDER: Senator Murphy.

MURPHY: Thank you, Mr. Chairman.

I hope you can understand our frustration around trying to divine the nature of this replacement plan.

I want to come back to this question of the conflict of interest issues that have been raised.

There's a great concern on behalf of the American people that this whole administration is starting to look like a bit of a get-rich-quick scheme; that we have a President who won't divest himself from his businesses and could potentially get rich off of them. We had a Secretary of Education who has big investments in the education space; a Secretary of Labor who could gut work protections and make a lot of money for his industry.

Earlier last year, [Centers for Medicare & Medicaid Services] announced a demonstration project that would have decreased incentives for physicians to prescribe expensive brand-name medications, and the drug companies that were affected immediately organized a resistance campaign.

Two days later, you announced your opposition to this demonstration project. One week later, you invested as much as $90,000 in a total of six pharmaceutical companies. All six, amazingly, made drugs that would have been impacted by this demonstration project. There are a lot of drug companies that wouldn't have been affected, but you didn't invest in any of those. You invested in six specific companies that would be harmed by the demonstration project.

Two weeks after that, you became the leader in Congress in opposition to this demonstration project.

And then guess what? Within two weeks of you taking the lead on opposition to that demonstration project, the stock prices for four of those six companies went up.

That's a damning timeline, Representative Price.

PRICE: Well, my opposition to having the federal government dictate what drugs are available to patients is long-standing. It goes back years and years. The fact of the matter is that I didn't know any of those trades were being made. I have a directed account broker, directed account.

The reason that you know about them is because I appropriately reported them in an ethical and appropriate manner as required by the House of Representatives.

MURPHY: But do you direct your broker around ethical guidelines? Do you tell him, for instance, not to invest in companies that are directly connected to your advocacy? Because it seems like a great deal as a broker. He can just sit back, take a look at...

PRICE: She.

MURPHY: ... the positions that you're taking.

PRICE: She can sit back.

MURPHY: She can sit back, in this case, look at the legislative positions you're taking, and invest in companies that she thinks are going to increase in value based on your legislative activities. And you can claim separation from that because you didn't have a conversation.

Why wouldn't you at least tell her, "Hey, listen, stay clear of any companies that are directly affected by my legislative work"?

PRICE: Because the agreement that we have is that she'd provide a diversified portfolio, which is exactly what virtually every one of you have in your investment opportunities.

MURPHY: But you couldn't have a diversified portfolio while staying clear of the six companies that were directly affected by your work on this issue?

PRICE: As I said, I didn't have any knowledge of those purchases.

MURPHY: Thank you, Mr. Chairman.

ALEXANDER: Thank you, Senator Murphy. Senator Warren.

WARREN: Thank you, Mr. Chairman.

Congressman Price, more than 100 million Americans now receive their healthcare through Medicare and Medicaid programs. These are seniors, people with disabilities, middle-class families who have parents in nursing homes, countless numbers of young children and they all benefit from these programs. So I want to understand the changes to Medicare and Medicaid that you have already proposed.

The budget that you recently authored as chair of the House Budget Committee would have cut spending on Medicare by $449 billion over the next decade. Is that right?

PRICE: I don't have the numbers right in front of me, but what we're trying…

WARREN: I have the numbers.

PRICE: Well, then I assume you're correct.

WARREN: All right.

PRICE: But we're…

WARREN: So you said you'd cut Medicare by $449 billion. Your FY '17 budget proposal also would have cut Medicaid funding that goes to the state governments by more than $1 trillion. Is that correct?

PRICE: I think, Senator, the – the – the metrics that we use for the success of these programs... *(Crosstalk)*

WARREN: ... dollars from Medicaid?

PRICE: What we believe is appropriate is to...

WARREN: Do you want me to read you the number out of this?

PRICE: No, I'm sure you're correct. What we believe is appropriate is to make certain that the individuals receiving the care are actually receiving care.

WARREN: I understand why you think you're right to cut it. I'm just asking the question. Did you propose to cut more than $1 trillion out of Medicaid over the next ten years?

PRICE: You have the numbers before you.

WARREN: Is that a yes?

PRICE: You have the numbers before you.

WARREN: I'll take it as a yes.

When President-elect Trump said I am not going to cut Medicare or Medicaid, do you believe he was telling the truth?

PRICE: I believe so, yes.

WARREN: Yeah, OK.

Given your record of proposing massive cuts to these programs, along with several other members of this committee, I sent the President-elect a letter in December asking him to clarify his position and he hasn't responded yet. So I was hoping you could clear this up.

Can you guarantee to this committee that you will safeguard President-elect Trump's promise and while you are HHS secretary, you will not use your administrative authority to carry out a single dollar of cuts to Medicare or Medicaid eligibility or benefits?

PRICE: What – what the questions presumes is that – that money is the metric. In my belief...

WARREN: I am asking about the money.

PRICE: ... from a scientific standpoint, if patients aren't receiving care, even though we're providing the resources, then it doesn't work for patients.

WARREN: Please, I'm sorry to interrupt, but we're very limited on time. The metric is money. And the quote from the President-elect of the United States was not a long discourse on this. He said he would not cut dollars from this program.

So that's the question I'm asking you. Can you assure this committee that you will not cut one dollar from either Medicare or Medicaid, should you be confirmed to this position?

PRICE: Senator, I believe that the metric ought to be the care that the patients are receiving...

WARREN: So, I take that as a no?

PRICE: I – it's – it's the wrong metric. We ought to be putting forth the resources...

WARREN: I – I'm not asking you whether or not you think you have a better metric. I'm asking you a question about dollars. Yes or no?

PRICE: What we ought to do is put forward the resources...
*(Crosstalk)*

WARREN: ... really simple questions. And frankly, the millions of Americans who rely on Medicare and Medicaid today are not going to be very reassured by your notion that you have some metric other than the dollars that they need to provide these services.

You know, you might want to print out President-elect Trump's statement, "I am not going to cut Medicare or

Medicaid," and post that above your desk in your new office because Americans will be watching to see if you follow through on that promise.

Now, I also would like to follow up on Senator Franken's question. Medicare was recently allowed to change the way that it pays hospitals for hip and knee replacements to something called a bundle. And that means Medicare pays a set price, and then the hospitals, not Congress, will decide the most effective implants. Now, I supported this change because the research shows that it really means you get better care at lower prices.

This in turn affects how much money the manufacturers of these hip and knee replacements can make. And one of the companies is Zimmer Biomet. They're one of the world's leading manufacturers of hips and knees and they make money if they can charge higher prices and sell more of their products.

The company knows this and so do the stock analysts. So on March 17, 2016, you purchased stock in Zimmer Biomet. Exactly six days after you bought the stock, on March 23, 2016, you introduced a bill in the House called the Hip Act that would require the [Health] secretary to *suspend* regulations affecting the [bundle] payment for hip and knee replacements.

Did you buy the stock, and then did you introduce a bill that would be helpful to the company you just bought stock in?

PRICE: The stock was bought by a direct – by a broker who was making those decisions. I wasn't making those decisions.

WARREN: OK. So you said you weren't making those decisions. These are your stock trades, though. They are listed under your name. Right?

PRICE: They are made on my behalf, yes.

WARREN: OK. Was the stock purchased through an index fund?

PRICE: I don't believe so.

WARREN: Through a passively managed mutual fund?

PRICE: No, it's a broker…

WARREN: To an actively managed mutual fund?

PRICE: It's a brokered directed account.

WARREN: Through a blind trust? So let's just be clear. This is not just a stockbroker, someone you pay to handle the paperwork. This is someone who buys stock at your direction. This is someone who buys and sells the stock you want them to buy and sell.

PRICE: Not true.

WARREN: So when you found out…

PRICE: That's not true, Senator.

WARREN: Well, because you decide not to tell them, wink, wink, nod, nod, and we're all just supposed to believe that?

PRICE: It – it – it's what members of this committee, it's the manner in which members of this committee… *(Crosstalk)* … But it's – it's important to appreciate that that's the case.

WARREN: When you found out that your broker had made this trade without your knowledge, did you reprimand her?

PRICE: What I did was comply…

WARREN: Did you fire her? Did you sell the stock?

PRICE: What I did was comply with the rules of the House in an ethical and legal and above board manner and in a transparent way. *(Crosstalk)*

WARREN: All right, let's just stipulate…

ALEXANDER: Time has expired, Senator Warren.

WARREN: I believe [another] Senator went over by two minutes. Did I misread the clock here?

ALEXANDER: By two minutes?

WARREN: I think that's what it was. And I just burned another fifteen seconds.

ALEXANDER: Well, keep burning them and you'll be up to two minutes.

WARREN: OK. So your periodic transaction report notes that you were notified of this trade on April 4, 2016. Did you take additional actions after that date to advance your plan to help the company that you now own stock in?

PRICE: I'm offended by the insinuation, Senator.

WARREN: Well, lemme just read what you did. You may be offended, but here's what you did. Congressional records show that *after* you were personally notified of this trade, which you said you didn't know about in advance, that you added 23 out of your bills, 24 co-sponsors.

That also, after you were notified of this stock transaction, you sent a letter to CNS calling on them to cease all current and future plan mandatory initiatives under the Center for Medicare & Medicaid Innovation. And just so there was no misunderstanding about who you were trying to help, you specifically mentioned...

ALEXANDER: Your two minutes are up, Senator Warren.
*(Crosstalk)*

WARREN: ... [hip] replacement.

ALEXANDER: Thank you. Senator Warren.

*Blackout. End of scene.*

## SCENE THREE – DR TOM PRICE

From the Senate Finance Committee's vote on
Congressman Tom Price's Nomination for Health
and Human Services Secretary
January 31, 2017

CHARACTERS

SEN. ORRIN G. HATCH, R-UTAH- CHAIRMAN

HATCH: I'm really disappointed that our Democrats on
the other side are deliberately boycotting this mark up.
Because [this] nominee is going to go through, regardless,
and, they didn't lay a glove on [him], as far as I was
concerned, during the hearings. They had a chance to ask
every question they wanted to ask, they were treated fairly,
I don't remember us treating their nominees this way.
I'm really disappointed at them boycotting Representative
Tom Price to be secretary of Health and Human Services.
We ought to be proud of him. And we ought to be willing
to support a man of integrity, which he is.

Now assuming that they can't support [him], then they can
vote against [him], and that's what an honest approach
to this matter would be. We're going to do this again
throughout the day to see if they will come and do the job
that they've been, they've been elected and sworn to do.
And I'm very disappointed in this type of crap. I mean,
my gosh. There's no excuse for it.

*Blackout.*

*Interval.*

# SCENE FOUR – DR TOM PRICE

From the Senate Finance Committee vote on
Congressman Tom Price's Nomination for Health
and Human Services Secretary
January 31, 2017

40 MINUTES LATER

CHARACTERS

SEN. ORRIN G. HATCH, R-UTAH- CHAIRMAN

HATCH: This is extremely disappointing to me, I have to say.
I always treat our colleagues on the other side who differ
with us with great respect and dignity so that they have
every opportunity to express themselves but you know
to not even come and express themselves! *(He laughs.)*
I mean, it's a dereliction of duty.

Now we'll keep the er, record open. And come back as
soon as we can get our colleagues to come and vote one
way or the other. With that, I think what we'll do is that
we'll recess until further notice. *(He bangs his gavel.)*

*Blackout. End of scene.*

## SCENE FIVE – SCOTT PRUITT

From the Senate Environment and Public Works Committee Nomination Hearing of the Alabama Attorney General Scott Pruitt for Administrator of the Environmental Protection Agency
January 18, 2017

CHARACTERS

*Panel Members:*
SEN. JOHN BARRASSO, R-WYO. CHAIRMAN
SEN. THOMAS R. CARPER, D-DEL. RANKING MEMBER
SEN. JAMES M. INHOFE, R-OKLA.
SEN. SHELDON WHITEHOUSE, D-R.I.
SEN. JEFF MERKLEY, D-ORE.
SEN. EDWARD J. MARKEY, D-MASS.
SEN. BERNARD SANDERS, I-VT.

*Witness:*
STATE ATTORNEY GENERAL SCOTT PRUITT, R-OKLA.

CARPER: Since coming to the Senate in 2001, I've opposed only one of the nominees for EPA administrator, supporting two Republicans, two Democrats nominees.

Too much of what I've seen of [Mr Pruitt's] record on the environment, and his views about the role of EPA are troubling, and in some cases, deeply troubling.

Even former Republican [Environmental Protection Agency Administrator Christine Whitman, recently said, and I quote, she "can't recall ever having seen an appointment of someone who is so disdainful of the agency and the science behind what the agency does."

It's hard to imagine a more damning statement, and from one who served not long ago in that position of trust, Mr. Pruitt, to which you've been nominated. Today is your opportunity to show that she's gotten it wrong. To be honest with you, coming to this hearing today, I fear that she's gotten it right. Thank you.

PRUITT: Good morning, Chairman Barrasso, Ranking Member Carper, members of the committee. It is an honor and a privilege to be before you today, to be considered for the position of EPA administrator.

When I ponder leading the EPA, I get excited about the great work to be done on behalf of our nation, in being a good steward of the natural resources we have as a nation. What could be more important than protecting our nation's waters, improving our air, and managing the land that we've been blessed with as a nation, all the while protecting the health and welfare of our people?

So if confirmed, I would lead the EPA with the following principles in mind. First, we must reject, as a nation, the false paradigm, that if you're pro-energy, you're anti-environment, and if you're pro-environment, you're anti-energy. I utterly reject that narrative. In this nation, we can grow our economy, harvest the resources God has blessed us with, while also being good stewards of the air, land and water by which we've been favored. It is not an either/or proposition.

Next, we should celebrate the great progress we've made as a nation since the inception of the EPA, but recognize that we have much work to do.

Third, rule of law matters. Process matters. It inspires confidence in those that are regulated. Regulators are supposed to make things regular, to fairly and equitably enforce the rules, and not pick winners and losers.

I seek to be a good listener, to listen, and to lead. You can't do one without the other. Listen...

*Protester interrupts proceedings*

Listen to those career staff at the EPA, as I've done as Attorney General of Oklahoma, and listen to you here in Congress, with respect to the needs of your respective states.

We should encourage open and civil discourse. One such issue where civil discourse is absent, involves climate change. Let me say to you, science tells us that the climate is changing, and that human activity, in some manner, impacts that change.

The ability to measure, with precision, the degree and extent of that impact, and what to do about it, are subject to continuing debate and dialogue, and well it should be. So with these principles in mind, I seek to answer your questions today.

Thank you, Mr. Chairman.

CARPER: Mr. Pruitt, you know, we don't often have the kind of disruptions in this room, and in this building, that we're witnessing here today.

And people might ask, well why – why are folks so concerned? And you'll have to go back to March 3rd, up in Detroit, Michigan, where President-Elect, then Candidate Trump, said these words.

"We're going to get rid of it, EPA, in almost every form. We're going to have little tidbits left, but we're going to take a tremendous amount out." That's what he said during the Republican primary.

And what did he say after the election? Well, November 10th, [on] Fox News with Chris Wallace, he said, "Environmental Protection, what they do is a disgrace. Every week they come out with new regulations."

And then Chris Wallace asked him, "Well who's going to protect the environment?" [President-elect Trump] responded to him and said, "Well, we'll – we'll be fine with the environment."

Well we're concerned that we won't be fine with the environment.

In you, he's put somebody in place who has actually defunded, or led to the defunding of the environmental protection unit within your own agency. And you've joined in a dozen or more lawsuits, over the last six years, ever since you've been [Oklahoma's] Attorney General, in going after the EPA.

Mercury.

PRUITT: I'm sorry?

CARPER: In 2011, the EPA required dirty coal power plants to clean up mercury and air toxic emissions by issuing the Mercury and Air Toxic Standards Rule.

This rule will reduce the mercury and neurotoxin that contaminates our stream, and our oceans, pollutes our fish and harms our children's health. As [Oklahoma's] Attorney General, you've been part of at least fourteen legal cases against the EPA, in at least three of these cases, against the EPA's rules to reduce mercury emissions from power plants.

Is that correct, just yes or no?

PRUITT: Senator, we have been involved in litigation around the Mercury and Air Toxic Standards Rule ......

CARPER: Is that correct, yes or no?

PRUITT: As I indicated, yes we've been a part of litigation...

CARPER: Thank you. It's my understanding that at least one of these cases against the mercury rule is still pending. Is that correct? Just yes or no.

PRUITT: I believe so, Senator. Yes.

CARPER: This position seems to question an EPA decision in 2000, in which the agency determined that "Mercury emissions from power plants pose significant hazards to public health and must be reduced," close quote.

Would you say the legal cases you've supported in the past directly challenged this agency finding? Yes or no.

PRUITT: Senator, the – the challenges we've had, as a – as a – as a state…

CARPER: Yes or no?

PRUITT: … along with the other states…

CARPER: Yes or no?

PRUITT: If I may, Senator – if I may.

CARPER: Just – just hold your fire. Just hold your fire.

PRUITT: OK.

CARPER: Are you aware that the last three administrators have publicly stated that the EPA is required to regulate mercury from power plants because of the health risks? Yes or no.

PRUITT: I believe that mercury should be regulated under Section 112.

CARPER: Thank you very much. My time is about to expire- I'll just hold it there.

BARRASSO: Thank you, Senator Carper.

Senator Inhofe?

INHOFE: Thank you, Mr. Chairman.

Well, I don't think you had adequate time to answer some of the questions that were asked. Is there anything you'd like to add, to elaborate on…

PRUITT: Yes, Senator. And thank you. I do want to say, to Senator Carper's concern, with respect to the President-elect's statements throughout the campaign, I believe there is a very important role for the Environmental Protection Agency. In fact, you and I talked about that in your office.

I believe that there are air quality issues, and water quality issues, that cross state lines, that the jurisdiction of the EPA is extremely important. And the EPA has served a very valuable role, historically.

After all, it was Republicans who created the EPA under executive order in the 1970. And we have much to celebrate.

BARRASSO: Senator Whitehouse.

WHITEHOUSE: Thanks, Chairman. Welcome to the committee, Mr. Pruitt.

One of the things I'd like to ask you about here is the connection between you and some of these fossil fuel companies. These are some of the companies that have supported you for [Oklahoma's] Attorney General, correct?

PRUITT: Yes, sir. I have a campaign committee that – yes.

WHITEHOUSE: And Devon Energy, Koch Industries, Exxon Mobil have all maxed out to that account…

PRUITT: I'm not aware if it's…

WHITEHOUSE: … at various times?

PRUITT: – maxed out or not, Senator, but they have – I'm sure they have given to the – to that committee.

WHITEHOUSE: You said to the Chairman that there is nothing that might place you in a conflict of interest that you have not disclosed. Yet you founded the Rule of Law Defense Fund, which is a dark money operation that supports the Republican Attorney Generals Association.

So very substantial funds have been solicited. Will you disclose your role in soliciting money and in receiving money for the Rule of Law Defense Fund?

PRUITT: Senator, a point of clarification. I actually did not start, nor initiate the Rule of Law Defense Fund. That is something I didn't…

WHITEHOUSE: You led it.

PRUITT: … do. I've been a – an officer of that organization…

WHITEHOUSE: OK.

PRUITT: … for 2016.

WHITEHOUSE: An officer of it.

PRUITT: There is an executive staff, fundraisers that actually carry out the functions of that organization. There are many attorneys general that serve on that board. It's not a decision of one. It's a decision of those that have been empowered to make those decisions.

WHITEHOUSE: But you haven't told us anything about that. You haven't told us…

PRUITT: I have no access…

WHITEHOUSE: … who you asked money…

PRUITT: That – that's a…

WHITEHOUSE: … from. You haven't told us what they gave, if you asked them. It's a complete black hole, into which, at least a million dollars goes. And based on your record of fundraising, it appears that a great deal of your fundraising comes from these organizations who are in the energy sector and devoted to fighting climate change.

PRUITT: Some of who – some of whom I've actually sued as well, Senator. But with respect to the role that…

WHITEHOUSE: Name one you've sued up there.

PRUITT: Exxon Mobil.

WHITEHOUSE: Really?

PRUITT: Yes.

WHITEHOUSE: My time has expired. We'll pursue this in further questioning.

PRUITT: Yeah. We're – we're involved, we are involved in – a situation in Oklahoma where multiple oil and gas companies, ConocoPhillips and others, have defrauded the state, in cleanup, with respect to spills that have occurred. And Exxon Mobil...

WHITEHOUSE: Yeah, it's a 'qui tam' fraud case. It has nothing to do with the environment.

PRUITT: Senator, I would – I would beg to disagree.

BARRASSO: I think we're going to reserve that for the second – for the second round.

WHITEHOUSE: I'm sorry. He was coming back to me, so I was responding. Thank you.

BARRASSO: Senator Merkley.

MERKLEY: Thank you, Mr. Chairman. Over a number of years, information started pouring into EPA that the estimate of the amount of fugitive methane escaping in gas and oil drilling, have been deeply underestimated. Gas companies didn't like this, because it presented a vision of natural gas being more damaging. Devon Energy is one of the groups that sought to cast doubt on this scientific information, and they came to you and they asked, will you be our mouthpiece in casting doubt, and send a letter we have drafted to the EPA? And you sent that letter.

And I just want to ask, first, are you aware that methane is approximately thirty times more potent than carbon dioxide as a global warming gas?

PRUITT: I am, Senator. It...

MERKLEY: Thank you.

PRUITT: The impact on human health...

MERKLEY: That's the – that's the answer. Yes. Thank you. It's a yes/no question. And on a one to ten scale, how concerned are you about the impacts of fugitive methane in driving global warming?

PRUITT: Methane, as you indicated, has a…

MERKLEY: One to ten scale, highly, ten, very concerned, or one, not so concerned?

PRUITT: The quantities of methane in the atmosphere, compared to $CO_2$ is less, but it's far more potent, and it is simple…

MERKLEY: Are you concerned? I'm asking about your level of concern.

PRUITT: Yes, yes.

MERKLEY: Highly concerned?

PRUITT: I'm concerned.

MERKLEY: Thank you. Do you acknowledge sending this letter to the EPA in October 2011?

PRUITT: Senator, that is a letter that's on my letterhead, that was sent to the EPA, yes, with respect to the issue…

MERKLEY: Do you acknowledge that 97% of the words in that letter came directly from Devon Energy?

PRUITT: I've not looked at the – the percentage of similar…

MERKLEY: The statement that's been analyzed many times is that all of the 1,016 words, except for thirty-seven words, were written directly by Devon Energy.

PRUITT: Senator, that was a step that I was taking as Attorney General, representing the interest of our state. Over 25% of our…

MERKLEY: Yes. So I didn't ask that question. I was just asking if you copied the letter, virtually word for word. You've acknowledged that yes – it's in the record. People can count it. It's correct.

So a public office is about serving the public. But you used your office as a direct extension of an oil company, rather than a direct extension of the interest of the public health of the people of Oklahoma.

Do you acknowledge that you presented a private oil company's position rather than a position developed by the people of Oklahoma?

PRUITT: Senator, I – with respect, I disagree. The efforts that I took as Attorney General were representing the interests of the State of Oklahoma.

MERKLEY: Thank you. What other environmental groups, or other groups, did you consult, so you had that full perspective before representing simply a for-profit oil company, using your official office and your official letterhead?

PRUITT: There – I – I consulted with other environmental officials in Oklahoma that regulate that industry, and learned from them, with respect to the concerns about the estimates that were provided by the EPA.

MERKLEY: Could you provide this committee with information showing who you consulted? Because the information that's in the public realm only shows that [Devon Energy] simply sent you a letter, asked you to send it, and you sent it, without questions. Why do you need an outside oil company to draft a letter when you have 250 people working for you?

PRUITT: Senator, as I've indicated, that was an effort that was protecting the state's interest in making sure that we made the voices of all Oklahomans heard on a very important industry to our state...

MERKLEY: ... all heard, but you only sent it on behalf of a single voice, the oil company.

Thank you.

BARRASSO: Senator Markey.

MARKEY: Thank you, Mr. Chairman. Donald Trump has called global warming a hoax caused by the Chinese. Do you agree that global warming is a hoax?

PRUITT: I do not, Senator.

MARKEY: So Donald Trump is wrong?

PRUITT: I do not believe that climate change is a hoax.

MARKEY: OK. That's important for the President to hear. Mr. Pruitt, you've made a career working on behalf of the fossil fuel industry to eviscerate regulations designed to protect public health and the environment. You have sued the EPA nineteen times to stop clean air and water protections.

Eight of those cases are still ongoing. Will you agree to recuse yourself from those lawsuits which you brought, as the Attorney General of Oklahoma, against the EPA for the entirety of the time that you are the administrator of the EPA?

PRUITT: With respect to pending litigation, the EPA ethics counsel has indicated, there will be an opportunity to get counsel from the EPA at that point, to determine what steps could be taken to avoid appearances of impropriety.

BARRASSO: Senator Sanders.

SANDERS: Thank you, Mr. Chairman. And I apologize for being late, but we were at a [nominee] hearing with Congressman Price, and perhaps [it's] not a great idea to have important nominating hearings at exactly the same time.

As you may know, some 97% of scientists have concluded that climate change is real. It is caused by human activity. And it is already causing devastating problems in our country and around the world. Do you believe that climate change is caused by carbon emissions, by human activity?

PRUITT: Senator, as I indicated – you weren't in here during my opening statement, but as I indicated the climate is changing, and human activity contributes to that in some manner.

SANDERS: In some manner?

PRUITT: Yes, sir.

SANDERS: 97% of the scientists who wrote articles in peer-reviewed journals believe that human activity is the fundamental reason we are seeing climate change. You disagree with that?

PRUITT: I believe the ability to measure with precision, the degree of human activity's impact on the climate is subject to more debate on whether the climate is changing or whether human activity contributes to it.

SANDERS: So you are applying for a job as administrator for the EPA, to protect our environment, and you're telling me that there needs to be more debate on this issue, and that we should not be acting boldly?

PRUITT: No, Senator. I – as I've indicated, the climate is changing. And human activity impacts that.

SANDERS: But you haven't told me why you think the climate is changing.

PRUITT: Well Senator, the job of the administrator is to carry out the statutes as passed by this body, and to comply with the...

SANDERS: Why is the climate changing?

PRUITT: Senator, in response to the CO2 issue, the EPA administrator is constrained by statutes...

SANDERS: I'm asking you a personal opinion.

PRUITT: My – my personal opinion is – is immaterial...

SANDERS: Really?

PRUITT: ... to the job of – to the job of carrying out...

SANDERS: You are going to be the head of the agency to protect the environment, and your personal feelings about whether climate change is caused by human activity and carbon emissions is immaterial?

PRUITT: Senator, I've acknowledged to you that the human activity impacts the...

SANDERS: Impacts?

PRUITT: Yes.

SANDERS: Scientific community doesn't tell us it impacts. They say it is the cause of climate change. Do you believe we have to transform our energy system in order to protect the planet for future generations?

PRUITT: I believe the EPA has a very important role in regulating the emission…

SANDERS: You didn't answer my question.

PRUITT: … of $CO_2$.

SANDERS: Do you believe we have to transform our energy system away from fossil fuel, to do what the scientific community is telling us, in order to make sure that this planet is healthy for our children and grandchildren?

PRUITT: Senator, I believe that the administrator has a very important role to perform in regulating $CO_2$.

SANDERS: Oklahoma has been subjected to a record-breaking number of earthquakes. Scientists say that Oklahoma's almost certain to have more earthquakes, and that the cause of this is fracking.

Can you point me to any enforcement actions you took against the companies that were injecting waste fracking water?

PRUITT: Senator, let me say, I'm very concerned about the connection between activity in Oklahoma and…

SANDERS: And therefore you must have taken action, I guess. Can you tell me who you fined for doing this, if you're very concerned?

PRUITT: The Corporation Commission in Oklahoma is vested with the jurisdiction. And they have actually acted on that.

SANDERS: And you have made public statements expressing your deep concern about this?

PRUITT: We have worked with – there are two…

SANDERS: You have made public statements – you're in a state which is seeing a record-breaking number of earthquakes. You're the Attorney General. Obviously, you have stood up and said you will do everything you can to stop future earthquakes as a result of fracking?

PRUITT: Senator, I've acknowledged that I'm concerned about…

SANDERS: You acknowledged that you are concerned?

PRUITT: Yes.

SANDERS: Your state's having a record-breaking number of earthquakes. You acknowledge you are concerned. If that's the kind of EPA administrator you will be, you're not going to get my vote.

BARRASSO: Senator Inhofe.

INHOFE: Mr. Chairman, I ask, at this point in the record – at this point in the record, that we reprint the Wall Street Journal op-ed piece that was written by two outstanding scientists, called "The Myth of the Climate Change 97%."

BARRASSO: Without objection. Senator Markey?

MARKEY: In your 2015 testimony before the House Science Committee, you wrote quote, "The EPA was never intended to be our nation's frontline environmental regulator. The states were to have regulatory primacy."

Will you support the statutory right of states to do more to reduce dependence on foreign oil, reduce global warming pollution, save money at the gas pumps, and create tens of thousands, hundreds of thousands of jobs in the clean car job business?

PRUITT: I think, Senator, generally the answer to that would be yes. I do respect and do believe that states have a very important role.

MARKEY: Do you support the current California waiver for greenhouse gas standards?

PRUITT: Senator, that's what would be evaluated and I think it's very difficult and we shouldn't prejudge the outcome in that regard if confirmed as administrator.

MARKEY: So, you're questioning the current waiver?

PRUITT: Well, the waiver is something that's granted on an annual basis and the administrator would be responsible for making that decision.

MARKEY: Yep. And so, you say you're going to review it?

PRUITT: Yes, Senator.

MARKEY: Yeah. And when you say review, I hear undo, you know, the rights of the states. It's troublesome, because we've heard how much you support state's rights when it comes to these issues.

So my problem really goes to this double standard that is created from the oil and gas industry perspective and you represent Oklahoma, you say they have a right to do what they want in the state of Oklahoma.

But when it comes to Massachusetts or California wanting to increase their protection for the environment, protect their – their victimization from carbon pollution, you say there, you're going to review.

BARRASSO: The Senator's time has expired.

*Blackout. End of scene.*

# SCENE SIX

From the Senate Judiciary Committee Nomination Hearing
of Senator Jeff Sessions for Attorney General
10 January, 2017

CHARACTERS

SEN. CHARLES E. GRASSLEY, R-IOWA,
CHAIRMAN
SEN. DIANNE FEINSTEIN, D-CALIF, RANKING
MEMBER
SEN. PATRICK J. LEAHY, D-VT.
SEN. LINDSEY GRAHAM, R-S.C.
SEN. RICHARD J. DURBIN, D-ILL.
SEN. SHELDON WHITEHOUSE, D-R.I.
SEN. AL FRANKEN, D-MINN.
SEN. CHRIS COONS, D-DEL.
SEN. TED CRUZ, R-TEXAS
SEN. MAZIE K. HIRONO, D-HAWAII

*Witness:*
SEN. JEFF SESSIONS, R-ALA., NOMINATED TO
BE U.S. ATTORNEY GENERAL

THREE PROTESTERS

GRASSLEY: Senator Sessions, before you are seated, I'd like
to administer the oath. Would you raise your hand please
and answer this question? Do you swear that the testimony
that you are about to give, before this committee, will be
the truth, the whole truth and nothing but the truth so help
you God?

SESSIONS: I do.

GRASSLEY: Thank you, and please be seated.

SESSIONS: It's an honor for me to be here, and to have my family with me. First, my wife Mary, my best friend for [nearly fifty] years, without her love none of this would have been possible for me and our family.

And we are so proud of our three children, each of which are here today. Mary Abigail Reinhardt, [and her husband Commanding Officer Paul Reinhardt]. They're now stationed in the Pacific Coast. They have two children, Jane Ritchie and Jim Beau.

My daughter, Ruth and her husband, John Walk have four children, Gracie, Hannah and Phoebe and Joanna who are twins.

My son, Sam, is a graduate of Auburn and Alabama Law School. Sorry, Sam, about the game the last night. Sam is an attorney in Birmingham and he is married to Angela Stratas. They have four children, Alexa, Sophia, Lewis and Nicholas. Ten grandchildren, the oldest is nine, and you can imagine the week we had at the beach this summer in Alabama.

Finally, I want to express how humbled I am to have received such overwhelming support and encouragement from our nation's law enforcement community, many are here today. Every major law enforcement organization in America has endorsed my candidacy.

I come before you today as a colleague, who's worked with you for years. You know who I am, you know what I believe in, you know that I'm a man of my word and can be trusted to do what I say I will do.

The Office of Attorney General of the United States is not a normal political office and anyone who holds it must have totally fidelity to the laws and the Constitution of the United States.

He or she must be committed to following the law. He or she must be willing to tell the President or other top officials if he or they overreach. He or she cannot be a mere rubber stamp.

Good policing and prosecutions over a period [of] years have been a strong force in reducing crime, making our communities safer. Drug use and murders are half what they were in 1980 when I became a United States attorney.

So I'm very concerned that the recent jump in violent crime and murder rates are not anomalies, but the beginning of a dangerous trend that could reverse those hard-won gains that have made America a safer and more prosperous place.

The latest FBI statistics show that all crime increased nearly 4% from 2014 to 2015. The largest increase since 1991, with murders increasing nearly 11%, the single largest increase since 1971. In 2016 there were 4,368 shooting victims in Chicago. In Baltimore, homicides reached the second highest per capita rate ever.

The country's also in the throes of a heroin epidemic, with overdose deaths more than tripling between 2010 and 2014 – tripling.

In recent years, law enforcement officers have been called upon to protect our country from the rising threat of terrorism that has reached our shores. If I'm confirmed, protecting the American people from the scourge of radical Islamic terrorism will continue to be a top priority.

Partnerships will also be vital to achieving much more effective enforcement against cyber threats, and the Department of Justice clearly has a lead role to play in that essential effort

I deeply understand the history of civil rights in our country and the horrendous impact that relentless and systemic discrimination and the denial of voting rights has had on our African-American brothers and sisters. I have witnessed it.

We must continue to move forward and never back.

I have an abiding commitment to pursuing and achieving justice and a record of doing that. And if confirmed, I will give all my efforts to this goal.

GRASSLEY: I want to thank you for your opening statement.

Now to the questioning.

The Attorney General of the United States is, of course, the nation's chief law enforcement officer.

Occasionally, you'll be called upon to offer an opinion to the President, who appointed you. You'll have to tell him, yes or no. And sometimes Presidents don't like to be told no. So I'd like to know, would you be able to stand up and say no to the President of the United States.

SESSIONS: Mr. Chairman, I understand the responsibility of the Attorney General. You simply have to help the President do things that he might desire in a lawful way and have to be able to say no.

GRASSLEY: Is it fair to say then, that regardless of what your position may have been as a legislator, your approach as Attorney General will be to enforce the law, regardless of policy differences.

SESSIONS: Absolutely Mr. Chairman

GRASSLEY: Some have expressed concerns about whether you can approach the Clinton matter impartially in both fact and appearance. How do you plan to address those concerns?

SESSIONS: Mr. Chairman, it was a highly contentious campaign. With regard to Secretary Clinton and some of the comments I made, I do believe that that could place my objectivity in question. I've given that thought.

I believe the proper thing for me to do, would be to recuse myself from any questions involving those kind of investigations that involve Secretary Clinton.

SESSIONS: Yes.

GRASSLEY: Senator Leahy

LEAHY: Thank you Mr. Chairman and welcome Senator Sessions and Mrs. Sessions.

Let's deal with the Violence Against Women Act [2013] that you voted against.

Spoke against it – you voted against it. That law expanded protections for some of the most vulnerable groups of domestic violence and sexual assault survivors, students, immigrants, LGBTQ victims and those on tribal lands. Why did you vote no?

SESSIONS: Mr. Chairman, a number of people opposed some of the provisions in that bill.

LEAHY: I'm just asking about you.

SESSIONS: I'm trying to answer.

LEAHY: Go ahead.

SESSIONS: So when we voted in the committee eight of the nine Republicans voted against the bill. One of the more concerning provisions was a provision that gave tribal courts jurisdiction to try persons who were not tribal members. That was the big concern that I raised on the legislation.

LEAHY: Well, on the tribal courts none of the non-Indian defendants that have been prosecuted have appealed to federal courts. Many feel it's made victims on tribal lands safer. Do you agree with that?

SESSIONS: Mr. Chairman, I do believe that the law has been passed by Congress, I'm interested to see how it plays out in the real world and I will do my best to make my judgment about how to enforce that as Attorney General.

Certainly the law itself has many powerful provisions that I'm glad was passed and that is in law and provides protections to women as victims of violence.

LEAHY: [In a] study last year, the FBI said that LGBT individuals were more likely to be targeted for hate crimes than any other minority group in the country. And in 2010, you stated expanding hate crime protections to LGBT individuals was unwarranted, possibly unconstitutional. You said the bill had been sent to cheapen the civil rights movement. Considering what the FBI has found, do you still feel that way?

SESSIONS: Mr. Chairman, the law has been passed. The Congress has spoken. You can be sure I will enforce it.

GRASSLEY: Senator Graham.

GRAHAM: Thank you, Mr. Chairman.

We're about to get an answer to the age-old question, can you be confirmed Attorney General of the United States over the objection of 1,400 law professors?

*Laughter.*

I don't know what the betting line in Vegas is, but I like your chances.

Now let's talk about issues.

As you know, me and the President-elect have had our differences about religious test. Would you support a law that says you can't come to America because you're Muslim?

SESSIONS: No.

GRAHAM: Would you support a law that says you say you're a Muslim and when we ask you, what does that mean to you? Well, that means I got to kill everybody that's different from me, it's OK to say they can't come.

SESSIONS: I think that would be a prudent decision.

GRAHAM: I hope we can keep people out of the country who want to kill everybody because of their religion. I hope we're smart enough to know that's not what most people in the Muslim faith believe.

SESSIONS: But it can be the religion of that person.

GRAHAM: That's right. That's the point we're trying to make here.

Immigration, you've said that the executive order of President Obama you believe is unconstitutional, the DACA [Deferred Action for Childhood Arrivals] law. You still have that position?

SESSIONS: I did for a number of reasons.

GRAHAM: I'm not, I mean…

SESSIONS: Right.

GRAHAM: I agree with you. Now, we've got 800,000 people have come out of the shadows. Will you advise the next President – President Trump, to repeal that executive order?

SESSIONS: It would certainly be constitutional, to end that order.

GRAHAM: Once we repeal it what do we do with the 800,000 kids who've come out of the shadows?

SESSIONS: Senator Graham, fundamentally we need to fix this immigration system. We've entered more and more millions of people illegally into the country. Each one of them produces some sort of humanitarian concern, but it is particularly true for children. So, we've been placed in a bad situation. I really would urge us all to work together.

I would try to be supportive…

GRAHAM: Would you prefer…

SESSIONS: … to end the illegality and put us in a position where we can wrestle with how to handle these difficult, compassionate decisions.

GRAHAM: Right. And the best way to do it is for Congress and the administration to work together and pass a law, not an executive order.

SESSIONS: Exactly.

GRAHAM: Do you support the continuation of Gitmo as a confinement facility for foreign terrorists?

SESSIONS: Senator Graham, I think it's designed for that purpose, it's a safe place to keep prisoners, we've invested a lot of money in that and I believe it should be utilized in that fashion and have opposed the closing of it. But as Attorney General…

PROTESTER: No! In the name of humanity…

GRAHAM: I just wanted to see if they were still listening.

TWO PROTESTERS: *(One female, one male):* No Trump! No KKK! No fascist USA! In the name of the humanity. No Trump! no KKK! No fascist USA!

GRAHAM: I think they're on the fence about Gitmo, but I'm not sure.

*Laughter.*

Cyber attacks, do you think the Russians were behind hacking into our election?

SESSIONS: I have done no research into that. I know just what the media says about it.

GRAHAM: Do you think you could get briefed any time soon?

SESSIONS: Well, I'll need to.

GRAHAM: I think you do too. You like the FBI?

SESSIONS: Do I like them?

*Laughter.*

GRAHAM: Yeah.

SESSIONS: Some of my best friends are FBI…

GRAHAM: Do you – do you generally trust them?

SESSIONS: Yes.

GRAHAM: Are you aware of the fact that the FBI has concluded that it was the Russian intelligence services who hacked into the DNC and Podesta's e-mails?

SESSIONS: I do understand that.

GRAHAM: From your point of view, there's no reason for us to be suspicious of them?

SESSIONS: Of their decision?

GRAHAM: Yeah.

SESSIONS: I'm sure it was honorably reached.

GRAHAM: How do you feel about a foreign entity trying to interfere in our election?

SESSIONS: I suppose, [it] goes in many ways to the State Department, our Defense Department, in how we as a nation have to react to that, that a price is paid.

GRAHAM: I agree, I've known you for, I guess, fifteen years now and we've had a lot of contests on the floor and sometimes we agree, sometimes we don't.

I'm from South Carolina so I know what it's like sometimes to be accused of being a conservative from the South, that means something other than you're a conservative from the South. In your case, people have fairly promptly tried to label you as a racist or a bigot or whatever you want to say.

How does that make you feel? And this is your chance to say something to those people.

SESSIONS: Well, that does not feel good.

PROTESTER: *(male)* This whole fascist regime needs to be stopped before they start.

PROTESTER: *(female)* No Trump! No Fascist USA

GRASSLEY: If nothing else, I'm clearing the room for you. Senator Durbin.

DURBIN: Thank you, Mr. Chairman.

When you came by my office last week, I talked to you about a man named Alton Mills. Alton, thank you for being here today. When Alton Mills was twenty-two-years-old, unemployed, he made a bad decision; he started selling crack-cocaine on the streets of Chicago.

He was arrested twice for possession of small amounts of crack-cocaine. The third time that he was arrested, the kingpins who had employed him turned on him, and he ended up being prosecuted under the three strikes and you're out law. At the age of twenty-four, he was sentenced to life without parole.

He had never been in prison before, and there were no allegations made against him other than possession and sale. No violence, no guns, nothing of that nature.

Alton Mills ended up spending twenty-two years in federal prison until December 2015 when President Obama commuted his sentence. He was finally able to go home to his family.

Senator Sessions, seven years ago, you and I co-sponsored a bill known as The Fair Sentencing Act that reduced the brutal sentencing disparity.

Inmates, overwhelmingly African-American, were spared thousands of prison years because of our joint effort to end this injustice, yet when I asked you to join Senator Grassley and me in permitting the almost 5,000 still serving under this unfair [law] to petition individually for leniency, you refused.

And you said "President Obama continues to abuse executive power in an unprecedented reckless manner to systemically release high-level drug traffickers and firearms felons. So-called low-level non-violent offenders simply do not exist in the federal system,".

Senator Sessions, Alton Mills and many more just like him do exist. So if you refuse to even acknowledge the fundamental injustice of many of our sentencing laws, why should you be entrusted with the most important criminal prosecution office in America?

SESSIONS: Senator Durbin, I think that's rather unfair.

I stepped out against my own Republican administration and said openly on the floor of the Senate that I believe that these crack cocaine laws were too harsh, and particularly it was disadvantageous to the African-American community.

You and I did not agree on the retroactivity because a lot of these were plea bargain cases and may not have been totally driven by the mandatory minimums.

DURBIN: Now, we have 5,000 prisoners sitting in federal prison still there and all I've asked and all Senator Grassley's asked, allow them as individuals to petition to the Department of Justice so that their sentences can be considered. That's something you've opposed.

SESSIONS: Well, I would tell you it's not the Attorney General's decision about when and where a mandatory minimum is imposed and whether it can be retroactively be altered. So I will follow any law that you pass.

DURBIN: Senator Sessions, since joining the Senate in 1997, you've voted against every immigration bill that included a path to citizenship for the undocumented. You described the DREAM Act, to spare children who are undocumented through no fault of their own, as quote, "a reckless proposal for mass amnesty."

You opposed the bi-partisan comprehensive immigration reform bill, which passed the Senate four years ago. You've objected to immigrants volunteering to serve in our armed forces, saying, quote, "In terms of who's going most likely to be a spy, somebody from Coleman, Alabama or somebody from Kenya."

When I asked what you would do to address the almost 800,000 undocumented children who would be subject to deportation if President Obama's executive order was repealed, you said, quote, "There is too much focus on people who are here illegally and not enough on the law."

Senator Sessions, there's not a spot of evidence in your public career to suggest that as Attorney General, you would use the authority of that office to resolve the challenges of our broken immigration system in a fair and humane manner. Tell me I'm wrong.

SESSIONS: Well, you are wrong, Senator Durbin. I'm going to follow the laws passed by Congress.

I do believe that if you continually go through a cycle of amnesty, that you undermine the respect for the law and encourage more illegal immigration into America. I believe the American people spoke clearly in this election.

GRASSLEY: Senator Whitehouse?

WHITEHOUSE: Senator Sessions, hello.

SESSIONS: Thank you, Senator Whitehouse.

WHITEHOUSE: As a question of law, does waterboarding constitute torture?

SESSIONS: Congress has taken an action now that makes it absolute improper and illegal to use waterboarding or any other form of torture in the United States.

WHITEHOUSE: Consistent with the wishes of the United States military.

SESSIONS: They have been supportive of that. And in fact, I'll just take a moment to defend the military. The military never… *(crosstalk)*

WHITEHOUSE: You don't need to defend them from me, I'm all for our military.

74

SESSIONS: I know, but so many people, think that the military conducted waterboarding. They never conducted any waterboarding, that was by intelligence agencies.

WHITEHOUSE: And General Petraeus sent a military wide letter disavowing the value of – of torture, as we – as we both know.

WHITEHOUSE: During the course of this boisterous political campaign, did you ever chant, "lock her up?"

SESSIONS: No I did not. I don't think. I heard it in rallies and so forth, sometimes I think humorously done. I think that probably is one of the reasons I believe that I should not make any decision about any such case.

WHITEHOUSE: And you understand that the good guy law man in the movies is the one who sits on the jailhouse porch and doesn't let the mob in?

SESSIONS: Exactly. Exactly.

WHITEHOUSE: So I'm from Rhode Island, as you know Senator. We have NAACP and ACLU members who've heard you call their organizations un-American.

We have a vibrant Dominican community who look at Big Papi, David Ortiz, swinging his bat for the Red Socks and wonder why you said, quote, "almost no one coming from the Dominican Republic to the United States is coming here because they have a provable skill that would benefit us."

And I've heard from police chiefs who worry that you, as Attorney General, will disrupt the community relations that they have worked hard over years of community engagement to achieve.

Is there anything you'd like to add now in our closing minute?

SESSIONS: Well, thank you. The – my comment about the NAACP arose from a discussion that I had where I expressed concern about their statements that were favoring, as I saw it, Sandinista efforts and communist guerrilla efforts in Central America.

SESSIONS: I said, in 1986, that NAACP represents one of the greatest forces for reconciliation and racial advancement in the country, probably number one. That's what I said then, I believed it and I believe it now.

GRASSLEY: Senator Franken?

FRANKEN: Thank you, Mr. Chairman.

In 2009, when you became the ranking Republican on this committee, you were interviewed. You said that moving forward, quote, "We're not going to misrepresent any nominee's record and we're not gonna lie about it," unquote. And we certainly don't wanna do that to our colleague. But I also think it's fair to expect that sitting before us today that you're not going to misrepresent your own record. That's fair to say, right?

SESSIONS: That is fair.

FRANKEN: OK.

So tell me, did you file twenty or thirty desegregation cases or is it some other number?

SESSIONS: Well, thank you, Senator Franken. It is important for us to be accurate. The records don't show that there were twenty or thirty actually filed cases. Some of the cases involved multiple defendants and multiple parties.

But the number would be less than that. So I...

FRANKEN: What – what do you think would've caused you to say...

SESSIONS: I don't know, I...

FRANKEN: ... that you filed twenty or thirty desegregation cases?

SESSIONS: Well, we had cases going throughout my district. And some of them were started before I came and continued after I left.

And so it was extraordinarily difficult to get a record by checking the docket sheet to find out exactly how many cases were involved. I heard one lawyer from the Department of Justice agreed with that large number...

FRANKEN: Let me move on...

SESSIONS: ... but I don't – that record doesn't justify it.

FRANKEN: The questionnaire you submitted for today asked you to list and describe the, quote, "ten most significant litigated matters you personally handled" – personally handled. And among the cases that you listed, that you personally handled, are three voting rights' cases and a desegregation case.

Last week, three attorneys who worked at DOJ and who actually brought three of the four cases wrote an op-ed piece in which they say, quote, "We can state categorically that Sessions had no substantive involvement in any of them."

Chairman Grassley, I would ask that that op-ed from last Tuesday's Washington Post be entered into the record.

GRASSLEY: Without objection, it will be entered.

FRANKEN: Are they distorting your record here?

SESSIONS: Yes. In fact, one of the writers there, Mr. Hebert, said I supported him in all the cases he brought; that I was more supportive than almost any other U.S. attorney; and that I provided office space. I signed the complaints that he brought.

FRANKEN: OK. Look, I'm not a lawyer, but it seems to me that a lawyer – if a lawyer has just his name added to a document here or a filing there, that lawyer would be misrepresenting his record if he said he personally handled these cases.

Two of the lawyers who wrote the op-ed have also submitted testimony for today's hearing – Mr. Gerry

Hebert and Mr. Joe Rich. Mr. Hebert says he, quote, "litigated personally two of the four cases" you listed. He said, "I can state with absolute certainty that Mr. Sessions did not participate in either." Mr. Rich worked on one of the four cases you listed. He said, quote, "I never met him at that time nor any other time, and he had no input to the case."

These represent three of the four cases that you claimed that were among the top ten cases that you personally handled.

So if you don't know [Mr Rich], it's hard for me to believe that you personally handled it.

SESSIONS: Well, when I found that – these cases, I had been supportive of them.

FRANKEN: You have filed…

SESSIONS: Mr. Hebert says, quote, "I have worked side by side with him on some cases in the sense that I have had to go to him for some advice," close quote.

FRANKEN: In some cases – not necessarily the ones you listed.

SESSIONS: Well, look, it was thirty years ago and my memory was my support for those cases.

FRANKEN: Your memory.

Our country needs an Attorney General who doesn't misrepresent or inflate their level of involvement on any given issue.

SESSIONS: Well, you are correct, Senator Franken. We need to be accurate in what we say. When this issue was raised, I did do a supplemental that said I "provided assistance and guidance to Civil Rights Division attorneys; had an open-door policy with them; and cooperated with them on these cases," close quote.

I did feel that they were national in scope and deserved to be listed on the form. If I'm in error, I apologize to you. I don't think I was.

FRANKEN: Well, you couldn't find twenty or thirty desegregation cases that you stated you had participated in. And you don't sound like you personally handled cases that you said you personally handled. Thank you.

SESSIONS: Well, I was on a radio interview without any records, and that was my memory at the time.

GRASSLEY: I think you answered the question.

FRANKEN: Thank you.

GRASSLEY: Senator Coons.

COONS: Thank you, Chairman Grassley. Welcome Senator Sessions.

Let me start with some questions about your time when you were Alabama Attorney General. At that point, Alabama was the only state in the country where a hitching post was used as a punishment for prisoners perceived as being unwilling to work or participate in the daily lives of the prison and they would be cuffed by both wrists to a pole at chest height, sometimes for seven, eight or nine hours unprotected from sun, heat or rain without access in some cases to water or even a bathroom. And as the Attorney General, you and the governor received letters from the U.S. Department of Justice telling you that Alabama's use of the hitching post in both men and women's prisons was unconstitutional and unjustified.

But as I understand it, the use of the hitching post continued throughout your term and you did not act to stop it. During this same period, the state of Alabama was sued not just about hitching posts, but also about chain gangs. Prison policies in Alabama said a man could be put on a chain gang if he failed to shave or keep his bed clean, if he disrespected a member of the staff and would end up doing hard labor breaking rocks while being chained together in groups of five, shackled with eight feet of chain between men.

And these practices were disproportionally affecting African-Americans. In later litigation, the practice of using the hitching post was called by an Alabama judge the most painful and torturous punishment in Alabama short of electrocution. And in 2002, the United States Supreme Court said using the hitching post was clearly unconstitutional when it was used in Alabama.

Can you please, Senator, tell me your view today of the use of the hitching post and chain gang in Alabama corrections and what your view is of what action you would take today if these practices were restored?

SESSIONS: Thank you very much, Senator.

That was an issue of the governor who campaigned and promised that prisoners should work and he was determined to make that happen.

After the Supreme Court ruling, I think it's crystal clear what the law is. That was disapproved and disallowed and found to be found unconstitutional and I would absolutely follow that as Attorney General.

COONS: In your view, did it take a ruling by the U.S. Supreme Court to clarify that this constituted torture, that it was just not bad corrections policy, it was actually substantively torture of prisoners?

SESSIONS: Senator Coons, I don't – I'm not – I don't recall ever personally being engaged in the studying of the constitutional issues at stake.

COONS: All your fellow Republicans on this committee, have supported meaningful reforms to address excessive mandatory sentences and incarceration, and in my experience here in six years with you, you have steadfastly opposed all of these efforts at bi-partisan sentencing reform.

SESSIONS: What we're seeing as a – beginning to see a rising crime, and the same time, a decline in sentences.

Sentences are down 19% already, as a based on *(inaudible)* and guidelines changes. So that's a matter of interest, and I felt we should slow down a bit before we go further…

COONS: Well if I might…

SESSIONS: … and make sure we're not making a mistake, Senator Coons.

GRASSLEY: Senator Cruz

CRUZ: Senator Sessions, congratulations on your nomination.

SESSIONS: Thank you.

CRUZ: You know, this has been an interesting day at this hearing, listening to Democratic senator after Democratic senator give speeches in praise of the rule of law. And I am heartened by that, I am encouraged by that, because for eight years, it's been absent.

For eight years we've seen a Department of Justice consistently disregarding the rule of law. When Eric Holder's Department of Justice allowed illegal gun transactions, illegally sold guns to Mexican gun traffickers, guns that were later used to murder border patrol agent Brian Terry, the Democratic members of this committee were silent.

PROTESTER: *(inaudible)* you are racist. You have tried to *(inaudible)*. You are – you caused *(inaudible)* organization. Black lives matter. Black lives matter. Black lives matter. Black lives matter.

CRUZ: You know, free speech is a wonderful thing.

When the Obama Justice Department sent millions of dollars of taxpayer money to sanctuary cities that were defying federal immigration law, the Democrats on this committee were silent. When the Obama administration refused to enforce federal immigration laws and unilaterally rewrote those laws, the Democrats on this committee were silent.

When the Obama administration released tens of thousands of criminal illegal aliens, including rapists and murderers, into the general population, Democrats on this committee were silent. When the Department of Justice signed off on the Obama administration paying a nearly $2 billion ransom to Iran contrary to federal law, the Democrats on this committee were silent.

And when the Obama administration released five Guantanamo terrorists without the required notification of Congress, the Democrats on this committee were silent. That pattern has been dismaying for eight years, but I take today as a moment of celebration. If once again this committee has a bipartisan commitment to rule of law that is a wonderful thing.

Now, if what was good for the goose were good for the gander, then a Republican Attorney General should be equally partisan, should disregard the law, should advance political preferences favored by the Republican party.

Senator Sessions, do you believe that would be appropriate for an Attorney General to do?

SESSIONS: No, I do not. I think we do have to be aware that when something like this is done I do believe it has a corrosive effect on public confidence in the constitutional republic of which we are sworn to uphold.

CRUZ: I think you are exactly right. I will say right now the reason I am so enthusiastically supporting your confirmation, is I have every degree of confidence you will follow the law faithfully and honestly.

GRASSLEY: Senator Hirono?

HIRONO: Thank you, Mr. Chairman. It's good to be back on this committee.

And aloha to you, Senator Sessions.

SESSIONS: Aloha.

HIRONO: I will do my best to be nice to you

SESSIONS: Well that won't be hard

HIRONO: Thank you very much.

Let me turn to the question of abortion. On Roe v. Wade, you did say quote, "I firmly believe that Roe v. Wade and its descendants represent one of the worst colossally, erroneous Supreme Court decisions of all time and it was an activists' decision."

My question is do you still hold that view?

SESSIONS: Well, I guess I've said that before, so I'm a pro-life advocate...

HIRONO: Thank you.

SESSIONS: ... but fundamentally, the problem, as I see it, with Roe versus Wade is that is denies the people [the] right to make laws that they might feel appropriate. Did the Supreme Court have that power? I concluded they didn't...

HIRONO: We can expect the make-up of the Supreme Court to change, and we can very well end up with a Supreme Court that will be very open to overturning Roe v. Wade. And should you be the Attorney General, would you direct or advise your solicitor general to weigh in, before that Supreme Court to repeal or to overturn Roe v. Wade?

SESSIONS: You're asking a hypothetical question. I just would not be able to predict what a well-researched, thoughtful response to – would be to manage it could happen in the future.

HIRONO: It's not just a hypothetical, but it is a real concern to a lot of people.

GRASSLEY: Senator Leahy.

LEAHY: Thank you, thank you, Mr. Chairman.

We had a dust-up in the press, as you recall, when Mr. Trump bragged about how he had grabbed women and so on. You, shortly after the tape came out, you said I don't characterize that as sexual assault.

But then you said later. "My hesitation is based solely on the confusion of the content of the 2005 tape when a hypothetical posed by the reporter, was asked in a chaotic post debate environment."

"And of course it's crystal clear that assault is unacceptable. I would never intentionally suggest otherwise." That's basically what you said after the confusion on your first comment. Is that correct?

SESSIONS: I believe that's correct.

LEAHY: Thank you. Is grabbing a woman by her genitals without consent, is that sexual assault?

SESSIONS: Clearly it would be.

LEAHY: If a sitting President or any other high federal official was accused of committing what the President-elect described in a context which it could be federally prosecuted, would you be able to prosecute and investigate?

SESSIONS: The President is subject to certain lawful restrictions, and they would be required to be applied by the appropriate law enforcement official if – if – if appropriate, yes.

LEAHY: And the conduct described would be sexual assault?

SESSIONS: Well, the confusion about the question, and it related to what was said on the tape. I did not remember at the time whether this was suggested to be an unwanted kind of...

LEAHY: OK, well let's...

SESSIONS: … would certainly meet the definition. If that's what the tape said, then that would be…

LEAHY: My – my question is very simple. Is grabbing a woman by her genitals without consent, is that sexual assault?

SESSIONS: Yes.

LEAHY: Thank you.

DURBIN: Senator Sessions, there's been a lot of controversy about refugees.

In the audience today is Omar al-Muktad [who] is a Syrian refugee. His story is a story of a journalist who for more than a decade publicized human rights abuses by the Assad regime, arrested seven times, imprisoned for two years. When he refused to stop writing after that, the prison guards broke his hands.

After his release from prison, he continued to write about the abuses of the Syrian security forces, he fled to Turkey. He was resettled in the United States by Catholic Charities after receiving refugee status.

During the course of the campaign there were some who said we should accept none, and many have questioned whether we should accept any refugees from anywhere.

One of your responsibilities as Attorney General will be the involvement of prosecutorial discretion, decisions that have to be made about the fate of men like Omar al-Muktad.

When it comes to cases like these in your role as the leading prosecutor in the United States of America, what is your feeling about your discretion to make the decision as to whether or not to spare individuals like those I've described?

SESSIONS: It's really the Secretary of State, usually through consultation with the President, that decides how many refugees should be admitted to the country.

Legally the president appears to have that power. But it would be my responsibility, I think, to make sure that it was exercised within the bounds of law.

GRASSLEY: Senator Franken.

FRANKEN: Senator Sessions, in late November President-elect Trump tweeted, quote, "In addition to winning the Electoral College in a landslide, I won the popular vote if you deduct the millions of people who voted illegally." Now, let's be clear. President-elect Trump lost the popular vote by more than 2.8 million votes, so what he's saying here is that more than 2.8 million fraudulent votes were cast. Do you agree with President Trump that millions of fraudulent votes were cast in the Presidential election?

SESSIONS: Senator Franken, I don't know what facts he may have had to justify his statement. I would just say that every election needs to be managed closely and I do believe we regularly have fraudulent activities occur during election cycles.

FRANKEN: Well, the Department of Justice is tasked with protecting voting rights and prosecuting fraud. So if millions upon millions of fraudulent votes were cast, I would imagine that the next Attorney General would be quite concerned about that. Did the President-elect tell you anything about what caused him to come to this conclusion?

SESSIONS: I have not talked to him about that in any depth or particularly since the election.

FRANKEN: Uh-huh. So he didn't share any evidence of voter fraud with you?

Before we move on, I should note for the record that state election and law enforcement officials surveyed in mid-December found virtually no credible reports of fraud among the nearly 138 million votes that were cast and no states reported indications of any widespread fraud.

What's truly troubling about these bogus claims of voter fraud, is they're routinely used to justify voter suppression. And thanks to the Supreme Court's disastrously decided Shelby County decision, which gutted the Voting Rights Act, it is easier than ever before for states to make it harder for people to vote.

Senator, do you still believe that there is little present-day evidence of states restricting access to the franchise? And if you do, what do you think the 4th Circuit got wrong when it found that North Carolina targeted black voters with almost surgical precision? Do you not believe that it was engaging in discriminatory conduct?

SESSIONS: I am not familiar with the details of the North Carolina law, but you are correct, any finding that's sustainable that there is a racial animus in the passing of a law that would restrict voting, that law could be unsustainable.

*[Editor's note: The following exchange came from the next round of questioning]*

FRANKEN: OK. CNN has just published a story, and I'm telling you this about a news story that's just been published. I'm not expecting you to know whether or not it's true or not, a story alleging that the intelligence community provided documents to the President-elect last week that included information that quote, "Russian operatives claimed to have compromising personal and financial information about Mr. Trump." These documents also allegedly say quote, "There was a continuing exchange of information during the campaign between Trump's surrogates and intermediaries for the Russian government."

Now, again, I'm telling you this as it's coming out, so you know. But if it's true, it's obviously extremely serious and if there is any evidence that anyone affiliated with the Trump campaign communicated with the Russian government in the course of this campaign, what will you do?

SESSIONS: Senator Franken, I'm not aware of any of those activities. I have been called a surrogate at a time or two in that campaign and I didn't have – did not have communications with the Russians, and I'm unable to comment on it.

FRANKEN: Very well. Without divulging sensitive information, do you know about this or know what compromising personal and financial information the Russians claim to have?

SESSIONS: Senator Franken, allegations get made about candidates all the time and they've been made about President-elect Trump a lot sometimes. Most of them, virtually all of them have been proven to be exaggerated and untrue. I would just say to you that I have no information about this matter.

FRANKEN: OK. Totally fair.

GRASSLEY: I want to thank everybody who participated including those in the audience.

Most importantly, thank you for your testimony today. You're eminently qualified to serve as Attorney General and I have every confidence that you're going to do a superb job.

Senator Sessions, you're excused.

*Blackout. End of scene.*

# SCENE SEVEN

From the Senate Judiciary Committee vote on
Senator Jeff Sessions for Attorney General
31 January, 2017

### CHARACTERS

SEN. CHARLES E. GRASSLEY, R-IOWA, CHAIRMAN
SEN. DIANNE FEINSTEIN, D-CALIF, RANKING
MEMBER
OTHER SENATORS – MEMBERS OF THE COMMITTEE

GRASSLEY: Good morning. Today, we're going to vote today on Senator Sessions' nomination to serve as Attorney General. Every Democrat on this committee, except for two that I know about, has already announced they intend to oppose the nominee. So, there isn't a lot of mystery here about how this thing may go today as far as the final vote's concerned.

Three weeks ago, Senator Sessions testified before this Committee for more than ten hours. Throughout that testimony, the American people had the opportunity to hear and learn directly from Senator Sessions what all of us on this Committee already knew to be true, because we have served with him for so long.

He told us he'll execute [the] role [of Attorney General] with strength, with integrity, and with independence in order to provide equal justice for all. That's precisely what we want in an Attorney General. Equal and fair application of the law.

I'm pleased to support his nomination and I'm pleased to cast my vote in favour of his confirmation, and I urge my colleagues to do the same thing.

With that, I'll turn to Ranking Member Feinstein.

SENATOR FEINSTEIN: Thank you very much, Mr. Chairman.

We have now had the opportunity to observe the first full week of the Trump administration. In that time, we've seen a flurry of Presidential declarations like none before. Some broad, some seemingly unconstitutional, some unenforceable, and all deeply concerning in their intent and legality.

Specifically, the President has issued six executive orders and ten Presidential memoranda or directives in the first week of his administration for a total of sixteen major administrative actions. Among these, the President has issued a sweeping order to undermine the Affordable Care Act, prohibited funding to any international aid group for simply providing information to patients about abortion, suggested a 20% tax on exports for Mexico to pay for a border wall, and most egregiously, issued multiple Executive orders on immigration. Not one order, idea, or pronouncement was meant to bring this country together. They only serve to tear the country further apart.

It's in this context with these events that we are being asked to consider this nomination. The President's nominee is well known for his positions and point of view. He has reinforced and supported the Trump mission, style, rhetoric, and views. He was the first Senator to endorse. He has attended at least forty-five Trump campaign events. He wore the hat. He was a leading voice and during the campaign he spoke at large rallies, smiling while crowds chanted 'lock her up". Then in October of last year, at one of the Presidential debates, and again at a rally in Virginia, candidate Trump repeatedly referenced him as my Attorney General. It is very difficult to reconcile the independence and objectivity necessary for the position of Attorney General with the partisanship this nominee has demonstrated. In fact just yesterday the Washington Post ran a story chronicling this nominee's involvement and connection to the President, his team, and their first acts. The Post declared the directives bore Trump's name, but another man's fingerprint, Jeff Sessions.

The Post went on to report that Senator Sessions, quote, lobbied for a shock and awe period of executive action that would rattle congress, impress Trump's base, and catch his critics unaware according to two officials involved in the transition planning, end quote. If this is true, how could we possibly conclude that this nominee will be independent?

The question is, if confirmed what will this nominee do? Will he support and defend these broad and destructive executive orders? Will he carry out and enforce the President's actions that may very well violate the constitution? If past is prologue to the future, it is not difficult to assess that he will.

According to the Washington Post, and again I quote, from immigration and health care, to national security and trade, Sessions is the intellectual godfather of the President's policies. Sessions' reach extends throughout the White House, with his aides and allies accelerating the President's most dramatic moves.

What will Senator Sessions do when faced with questions on reproductive rights? This is an issue of real importance to a dominant majority of women in this country. At his hearing asked directly if it is still his view that Roe v. Wade is quote "one of the worst colossally erroneous Supreme Court decisions of all time"? end quote. He said, quote, "It is", end quote. He said he will, quote, "respect", end quote, Roe v. Wade, but believes the decision, quote, "violated the Constitution," end quote.

The final issue I would like to touch on, Mr. Chairman, is civil liberties. Ever since 9/11, we had an intense struggle between civil liberties and national security. I think people know I believe in strong national security. But also believe we must never sacrifice our values or fundamental constitutional rights as Americans. It is clear, from the record, the nominee believes otherwise. Senator Sessions was one of only nine senators in 2005 to vote against the Detainee Treatment Act, which contains Senator McCain's and my bipartisan amendment that prohibited cruel, inhumane and degrading punishment for individuals in American custody. In 2008, on the Senate floor, he claimed that enhanced interrogation techniques were necessary to stop additional terrorist plots.

As the Senate Intelligence Committee's extensive study revealed, the so-called enhanced interrogation techniques, particularly waterboarding, were and are ineffective and did not produce actionable intelligence, and in 2016 the nominee was one of twenty-one senators to vote against prohibiting waterboarding. He has even expressed support for the detention of Americans captured on American soil to be held without charge or trial.

These positions give me no confidence the nominee will uphold our laws and civil liberties as Attorney General. Mr Chairman we're being asked to vote on a nominee that will have to stand up to a President who is clearly willing to ignore the law, and even issue orders in violation of the constitution. We are are being asked to determine whether this nominee's record demonstrates that he will have the objectivity to enforce the law for all Americans, and be an independent Attorney General, and not an arm of the White House.

Yesterday, early in the evening, we clearly saw what a truly independent Attorney General does. Sally Yates, the acting Attorney General declared that under her leadership the department could not defend Trump's executive order on immigrants and refugees. Here's what she wrote, "My responsibility is to ensure that the position of the Department of Justice is not only legally defensible, but is informed by our best view of what the law is after consideration of all of the facts. At present, I am not convinced that the events of the Executive order is consistent with these responsibilities, nor am I convinced that the executive order is lawful. Consequently, for as long as I am the Attorney General, the Department of Justice will not present arguments in defense of the executive order unless and until I become convinced that it is appropriate to do so."

Members, that statement took guts. That statement said what an independent Attorney General should do. That statement took a steel spine to stand up and say no. It took the courage of Elliott Richardson and William Ruckelshaus who stood up to President Nixon.

This is what an Attorney General must be willing and able to do.

I have no confidence that Senator Sessions will do that.

With this in mind, I must vote no. Thank you.

*Blackout.*

*A recording of the Senate roll call and vote on Senator Jeff Sessions' nomination as Attorney General is played as the audience leave the auditorium.*